Using
Web-Based
Tools

in the English Language Arts Classroom

Susan Brooks-Young

WALCH EDUCATION®

1   2   3   4   5   6   7   8   9   10

ISBN 978-0-8251-6598-6

Copyright © 2010

J. Weston Walch, Publisher

40 Walch Drive • Portland, ME 04103

www.walch.com

Printed in the United States of America

Table of Contents

To the Teacher

The goal of this book is to get your students excited about English Language Arts activities by leveraging their interest in online tools for collaboration. In addition, students who complete these activities will employ a number of skills directly related to academic standards and 21st century learning.

Increasing numbers of employers expect to hire staff who are skilled in using tools to create and share online content for a wide range of purposes. Your students have probably used one or more of these tools outside of school, but figuring out basic features does not ensure that students will also develop the skills they need to collaborate effectively. Students aren't likely to understand appropriate work-related use of these tools without adult guidance. This book introduces four different Web-based tools—wikis, blogs, Web-based word processors, and Web-based presentations. These technologies were chosen because they promote development of workplace skills and support engaging activities that encourage students to perform well academically.

Each tool is featured in five activities. You may choose to use some or all of these activities. You will find that each wiki and blog activity can stand alone, but the lessons at the end of these sections are best done if many of the earlier activities have been completed. The first two Web-based word processing activities and the first and last Web-based presentation activities are also stand-alone; however, the remaining lessons in both of these sections are most effective if used in sequence.

Most of the activities are meant to be finished in a single class period, although some can be made as detail-oriented as possible and can be spread across a few classes. The material covered would fit well into a general English Language Arts class; many activities are also suitable for other courses that require students to engage in writing activities or share presentations.

The following correlation charts for the activities in this book connect each activity to the IRA/NCTE Standards, ISTE's National Education Technology Standards for Students (NETS*S), and the Framework for 21st Century Learning from the Partnership for 21st Century Skills. There is also a general rubric to help you with assessment. Properly used, this book can be a fun way to help students meet the high academic standards of today's classroom.

Correlations to Standards for Wiki Activities

Activity	IRA/NCTE	NETS*S	Framework for 21st Century Learning	Description
1. Working in a Wiki	**Standard 8**—Students use a variety of technological and information resources (e.g., libraries, databases, computer networks, video) to gather and synthesize information and to create and communicate knowledge.	**Standard 6. Technology Operations and Concepts**—Students demonstrate a sound understanding of technology concepts, systems, and operations.	**ICT Literacy**—Use technology as a tool to research, organize, evaluate and communicate information.	This activity introduces students to a class wiki where they practice the basic skills needed to access and contribute to the wiki.
2. Literary Analysis—21st Century Style	**Standard 3**—Students apply a wide range of strategies to comprehend, interpret, evaluate, and appreciate texts. They draw on their prior experience, their interactions with other readers and writers, their knowledge of word meaning and of other texts, their word identification strategies, and their understanding of textual features (e.g., sound-letter correspondence, sentence structure, context, graphics). **Standard 8**—Students use a variety of technological and information resources (e.g., libraries, databases, computer networks, video) to gather and synthesize information and to create and communicate knowledge.	**Standard 4. Critical Thinking, Problem Solving, and Decision Making**—Students use critical thinking skills to plan and conduct research, manage projects, solve problems, and make informed decisions using appropriate digital tools and resources. **Standard 6. Technology Operations and Concepts**—Students demonstrate a sound understanding of technology concepts, systems, and operations.	**Core Subjects and 21st Century Themes**—Mastery of core subjects and 21st century themes is essential for students in the 21st century. **ICT Literacy**—Use technology as a tool to research, organize, evaluate and communicate information.	In this small-group activity, students contribute to a class analysis of a work of fiction using a class wiki.
3. Build Your Own Reference Library—Glossary of Terms	**Standard 3**—Students apply a wide range of strategies to comprehend, interpret, evaluate, and appreciate texts. They draw on their prior experience, their interactions with other readers and writers, their knowledge of word meaning and of other texts, their word identification strategies, and their understanding of textual features (e.g., sound-letter correspondence, sentence structure, context, graphics). **Standard 8**—Students use a variety of technological and information resources (e.g., libraries, databases, computer networks, video) to gather and synthesize information and to create and communicate knowledge.	**Standard 2. Communication and Collaboration**—Students use digital media and environments to communicate and work collaboratively, including at a distance, to support individual learning and contribute to the learning of others. **Standard 3. Research and Information Fluency**—Students apply digital tools to gather, evaluate, and use information.	**Communication and Collaboration**—Assume shared responsibility for collaborative work, and value the individual contributions made by each team member. **Information Literacy**—Access and evaluate information.	In this small-group activity, students create a glossary of terms using a class wiki.

4. **Build Your Own Reference Library— Formatting and Style Guide**	**Standard 4**—Students adjust their use of spoken, written, and visual language (e.g., conventions, style, vocabulary) to communicate effectively with a variety of audiences and for different purposes. **Standard 8**—Students use a variety of technological and information resources (e.g., libraries, databases, computer networks, video) to gather and synthesize information and to create and communicate knowledge.	**Standard 2. Communication and Collaboration**—Students use digital media and environments to communicate and work collaboratively, including at a distance, to support individual learning and contribute to the learning of others. **Standard 3. Research and Information Fluency**—Students apply digital tools to gather, evaluate, and use information.	**Communication and Collaboration**—Assume shared responsibility for collaborative work, and value the individual contributions made by each team member. **Information Literacy**—Access and evaluate information.	In this small-group activity, students create a formatting and style guide using a class wiki.
5. **Read All About It**	**Standard 8**—Students use a variety of technological and information resources (e.g., libraries, databases, computer networks, video) to gather and synthesize information and to create and communicate knowledge. **Standard 12**—Students use spoken, written, and visual language to accomplish their own purposes (e.g., for learning, enjoyment, persuasion, and the exchange of information).	**Standard 2. Communication and Collaboration**—Students use digital media and environments to communicate and work collaboratively, including at a distance, to support individual learning and contribute to the learning of others.	**Communication and Collaboration**—Articulate thoughts and ideas effectively using oral, written and nonverbal communication skills in a variety of forms and contexts. **Communication and Collaboration**—Use communication for a range of purposes (e.g., to inform, instruct, motivate, and persuade).	Students write and post online book reviews and comment on one another's work.

Correlations to Standards for Blog Activities				
Activity	IRA/NCTE	NETS*S	Framework for 21st Century Learning	Description
6. Working in a Blog	**Standard 8**—Students use a variety of technological and information resources (e.g., libraries, databases, computer networks, video) to gather and synthesize information and to create and communicate knowledge.	**Standard 6. Technology Operations and Concepts**—Students demonstrate a sound understanding of technology concepts, systems, and operations.	**ICT Literacy**—Use technology as a tool to research, organize, evaluate and communicate information.	This activity introduces students to a class blog where they practice the basic skills needed to access and contribute to the blog.
7. Poetry Anthology	**Standard 6**—Students apply knowledge of language structure, language conventions (e.g., spelling and punctuation), media techniques, figurative language, and genre to create, critique, and discuss print and non-print texts. **Standard 8**—Students use a variety of technological and information resources (e.g., libraries, databases, computer networks, video) to gather and synthesize information and to create and communicate knowledge.	**Standard 1. Creativity and Innovation**—Students demonstrate creative thinking, construct knowledge, and develop innovative products and processes using technology. **Standard 6. Technology Operations and Concepts**—Students demonstrate a sound understanding of technology concepts, systems, and operations.	**Core Subjects and 21st Century Themes**—Mastery of core subjects and 21st century themes is essential for students in the 21st century. **ICT Literacy**—Use technology as a tool to research, organize, evaluate and communicate information.	Students use the class blog to create an interactive online poetry anthology.
8. What a Character!	**Standard 3**—Students apply a wide range of strategies to comprehend, interpret, evaluate, and appreciate texts. They draw on their prior experience, their interactions with other readers and writers, their knowledge of word meaning and of other texts, their word identification strategies, and their understanding of textual features (e.g., sound-letter correspondence, sentence structure, context, graphics). **Standard 8**—Students use a variety of technological and information resources (e.g., libraries, databases, computer networks, video) to gather and synthesize information and to create and communicate knowledge.	**Standard 1. Creativity and Innovation**—Students demonstrate creative thinking, construct knowledge, and develop innovative products and processes using technology. **Standard 2. Communication and Collaboration**—Students use digital media and environments to communicate and work collaboratively, including at a distance, to support individual learning and contribute to the learning of others.	**Communication and Collaboration**—Articulate thoughts and ideas effectively using oral, written and nonverbal communication skills in a variety of forms and contexts. **Creativity and Innovation**—Be open and responsive to new and diverse perspectives; incorporate group input and feedback into the work.	Students use the class blog to explore a character from a work of fiction being read for class.

9. Book Study	**Standard 3**—Students apply a wide range of strategies to comprehend, interpret, evaluate, and appreciate texts. They draw on their prior experience, their interactions with other readers and writers, their knowledge of word meaning and of other texts, their word identification strategies, and their understanding of textual features (e.g., sound-letter correspondence, sentence structure, context, graphics). **Standard 8**—Students use a variety of technological and information resources (e.g., libraries, databases, computer networks, video) to gather and synthesize information and to create and communicate knowledge.	**Standard 1. Creativity and Innovation**—Students demonstrate creative thinking, construct knowledge, and develop innovative products and processes using technology. **Standard 2. Communication and Collaboration**—Students use digital media and environments to communicate and work collaboratively, including at a distance, to support individual learning and contribute to the learning of others.	**Communication and Collaboration**—Articulate thoughts and ideas effectively using oral, written and nonverbal communication skills in a variety of forms and contexts. **Creativity and Innovation**—Be open and responsive to new and diverse perspectives; incorporate group input and feedback into the work.	Students use the class blog to participate in an online book study as they read a work of nonfiction for class.
10. Interactive News	**Standard 3**—Students apply a wide range of strategies to comprehend, interpret, evaluate, and appreciate texts. They draw on their prior experience, their interactions with other readers and writers, their knowledge of word meaning and of other texts, their word identification strategies, and their understanding of textual features (e.g., sound-letter correspondence, sentence structure, context, graphics). **Standard 8**—Students use a variety of technological and information resources (e.g., libraries, databases, computer networks, video) to gather and synthesize information and to create and communicate knowledge.	**Standard 1. Creativity and Innovation**—Students demonstrate creative thinking, construct knowledge, and develop innovative products and processes using technology. **Standard 2. Communication and Collaboration**—Students use digital media and environments to communicate and work collaboratively, including at a distance, to support individual learning and contribute to the learning of others.	**Communication and Collaboration**—Articulate thoughts and ideas effectively using oral, written and nonverbal communication skills in a variety of forms and contexts. **Creativity and Innovation**—Be open and responsive to new and diverse perspectives; incorporate group input and feedback into the work. **Information Literacy**—Evaluate information critically and competently.	Students review and evaluate comments about an online news story posted by readers of a commercial or professional blog.

Correlations to Standards for Web-Based Word Processing Activities

Activity	IRA/NCTE	NETS*S	Framework for 21st Century Learning	Description
11. Using a Web-Based Word Processor	**Standard 8**—Students use a variety of technological and information resources (e.g., libraries, databases, computer networks, video) to gather and synthesize information and to create and communicate knowledge.	**Standard 6. Technology Operations and Concepts**—Students demonstrate a sound understanding of technology concepts, systems, and operations.	**ICT Literacy**—Use technology as a tool to research, organize, evaluate and communicate information.	This activity introduces students to a Web-based word processor where they practice the basic skills needed to create, edit, and share documents.
12. Collaborative Notes	**Standard 3**—Students apply a wide range of strategies to comprehend, interpret, evaluate, and appreciate texts. They draw on their prior experience, their interactions with other readers and writers, their knowledge of word meaning and of other texts, their word identification strategies, and their understanding of textual features (e.g., sound-letter correspondence, sentence structure, context, graphics). **Standard 8**—Students use a variety of technological and information resources (e.g., libraries, databases, computer networks, video) to gather and synthesize information and to create and communicate knowledge.	**Standard 2. Communication and Collaboration**—Students use digital media and environments to communicate and work collaboratively, including at a distance, to support individual learning and contribute to the learning of others. **Standard 3. Research and Information Fluency**—Students apply digital tools to gather, evaluate, and use information.	**Communication and Collaboration**—Demonstrate ability to work effectively and respectfully with diverse teams. **Use and Manage Information**—Manage the flow of information from a wide variety of sources.	Students work in study groups to create an online document used for collaborative note-taking.
13. Writing a Mini-Essay	**Standard 4**—Students adjust their use of spoken, written, and visual language (e.g., conventions, style, vocabulary) to communicate effectively with a variety of audiences and for different purposes. **Standard 8**—Students use a variety of technological and information resources (e.g., libraries, databases, computer networks, video) to gather and synthesize information and to create and communicate knowledge.	**Standard 2. Communication and Collaboration**—Students use digital media and environments to communicate and work collaboratively, including at a distance, to support individual learning and contribute to the learning of others.	**Communication and Collaboration**—Articulate thoughts and ideas effectively using oral, written and nonverbal communication skills in a variety of forms and contexts.	Students write a two- to three-paragraph mini-essay using a Web-based word processor.
14. Peer Editing a Mini-Essay	**Standard 3**—Students apply a wide range of strategies to comprehend, interpret, evaluate, and appreciate texts. They draw on their prior experience, their interactions with other readers and writers, their knowledge of word meaning and of other texts, their word identification strategies, and their understanding of textual features (e.g., sound-letter correspondence, sentence structure, context, graphics). **Standard 8**—Students use a variety of technological and information resources (e.g., libraries, databases, computer networks, video) to gather and synthesize information and to create and communicate knowledge.	**Standard 2. Communication and Collaboration**—Students use digital media and environments to communicate and work collaboratively, including at a distance, to support individual learning and contribute to the learning of others.	**Communication and Collaboration**—Demonstrate ability to work effectively and respectfully with diverse teams. **Flexibility and Adaptability**—Incorporate feedback effectively and deal positively with praise, setbacks and criticism.	Students use the collaborative features of a Web-based word processing document to peer-edit mini-essays.

| 15. Revising a Mini-Essay | Standard 3—Students apply a wide range of strategies to comprehend, interpret, evaluate, and appreciate texts. They draw on their prior experience, their interactions with other readers and writers, their knowledge of word meaning and of other texts, their word identification strategies, and their understanding of textual features (e.g., sound-letter correspondence, sentence structure, context, graphics).

Standard 8—Students use a variety of technological and information resources (e.g., libraries, databases, computer networks, video) to gather and synthesize information and to create and communicate knowledge. | Standard 2. Communication and Collaboration—Students use digital media and environments to communicate and work collaboratively, including at a distance, to support individual learning and contribute to the learning of others. | Communication and Collaboration—Demonstrate ability to work effectively and respectfully with diverse teams.

Flexibility and Adaptability—Incorporate feedback effectively and deal positively with praise, setbacks and criticism. | Students use feedback provided by online collaborators as they revise mini-essays they have written. |

Correlations to Standards for Web-Based Presentation Activities

Activity	IRA/NCTE	NETS*S	Framework for 21st Century Learning	Description
16. Using a Web-Based Presentation Tool	**Standard 8**—Students use a variety of technological and information resources (e.g., libraries, databases, computer networks, video) to gather and synthesize information and to create and communicate knowledge.	**Standard 6. Technology Operations and Concepts**—Students demonstrate a sound understanding of technology concepts, systems, and operations.	**ICT Literacy**—Use technology as a tool to research, organize, evaluate and communicate information.	This activity introduces students to a Web-based presentation tool where they practice the basic skills needed to create, edit, and share online presentations.
17. Planning a Web-Based Presentation— Brainstorming	**Standard 5**—Students employ a wide range of strategies as they write and use different writing process elements appropriately to communicate with different audiences for a variety of purposes. **Standard 8**—Students use a variety of technological and information resources (e.g., libraries, databases, computer networks, video) to gather and synthesize information and to create and communicate knowledge.	**Standard 2. Communication and Collaboration**—Students use digital media and environments to communicate and work collaboratively, including at a distance, to support individual learning and contribute to the learning of others. **Standard 3. Research and Information Fluency**—Students apply digital tools to gather, evaluate, and use information.	**Communication and Collaboration**—Demonstrate ability to work effectively and respectfully with diverse teams. **Use and Manage Information**—Manage the flow of information from a wide variety of sources.	Students collaborate in small working groups to brainstorm ideas for an online presentation.
18. Planning a Web-Based Presentation— Outlining	**Standard 5**—Students employ a wide range of strategies as they write and use different writing process elements appropriately to communicate with different audiences for a variety of purposes. **Standard 8**—Students use a variety of technological and information resources (e.g., libraries, databases, computer networks, video) to gather and synthesize information and to create and communicate knowledge.	**Standard 2. Communication and Collaboration**—Students use digital media and environments to communicate and work collaboratively, including at a distance, to support individual learning and contribute to the learning of others. **Standard 3. Research and Information Fluency**—Students apply digital tools to gather, evaluate, and use information.	**Communication and Collaboration**—Demonstrate ability to work effectively and respectfully with diverse teams. **Use and Manage Information**—Manage the flow of information from a wide variety of sources.	Students collaborate in small working groups to outline an online presentation.

19. Planning a Web-Based Presentation—Images and Text	**Standard 5**—Students employ a wide range of strategies as they write and use different writing process elements appropriately to communicate with different audiences for a variety of purposes. **Standard 8**—Students use a variety of technological and information resources (e.g., libraries, databases, computer networks, video) to gather and synthesize information and to create and communicate knowledge.	**Standard 2. Communication and Collaboration**—Students use digital media and environments to communicate and work collaboratively, including at a distance, to support individual learning and contribute to the learning of others. **Standard 3. Research and Information Fluency**—Students apply digital tools to gather, evaluate, and use information.	**Communication and Collaboration**—Demonstrate ability to work effectively and respectfully with diverse teams. **Use and Manage Information**—Manage the flow of information from a wide variety of sources.	Students collaborate in small working groups to write a short presentation script and then add content to each slide.
20. Six-Word Stories	**Standard 4**—Students adjust their use of spoken, written, and visual language (e.g., conventions, style, vocabulary) to communicate effectively with a variety of audiences and for different purposes. **Standard 8**—Students use a variety of technological and information resources (e.g., libraries, databases, computer networks, video) to gather and synthesize information and to create and communicate knowledge.	**Standard 1. Creativity and Innovation**—Students demonstrate creative thinking, construct knowledge, and develop innovative products and processes using technology. **Standard 2. Communication and Collaboration**—Students use digital media and environments to communicate and work collaboratively, including at a distance, to support individual learning and contribute to the learning of others.	**Communication and Collaboration**—Demonstrate ability to work effectively and respectfully with diverse teams.	Students collaborate in small working groups to write and publish an online presentation consisting of one 6-word story per group member.

General Rubric

When assessing student work for which you are evaluating performance in terms of knowledge and applied skills, you may want to use a rubric to guide scoring. The following rubric provides a sample of the areas and criteria that may be appropriate to review; however, it is unlikely that you would include all the areas shown here. Pick and choose those areas most appropriate for a specific activity.

	Percent of grade	4 (Excellent)	3 (Good)	2 (Fair)	1 (Poor)
Content knowledge and technology skills specific to assignment		Response and comments are consistently reasonable to exceed expectations for the assignment. Actively uses technology skills, and transfers them to other situations and contexts.	Majority of the response and/or comments are reasonable. Majority of technology skills or methods are applied correctly. Student sometimes transfers them to other situations or contexts.	Response and/or comments are confusing or incorrect. Some technology skills are used correctly.	No evidence of knowledge or technology skill development. Few correct methods; few correct answers.
Research		Work shows high-quality research on topic or theme. Research is used consistently to support main claims or points. Sources are reputable and cited correctly.	Work reflects solid research. Research is used to support most main claims or points. Sources are reputable and cited correctly.	There is little evidence of research, or research is used inconsistently to support claims or points. Citations are incorrect or incomplete. Sources are questionable.	There is no evidence of research. No citations are provided.
Grammar, spelling, and punctuation		Excellent use of mechanics. Sentences are varied and well-constructed. Student reviews work methodically for errors.	Uses mechanics consistently. Some variety in sentence construction. Student reviewed work for errors.	Inconsistent control of mechanics. Student reviewed work for errors.	Several errors. Little or no attempt to check work.
Writing		Purpose or argument is focused, well-presented, and insightful. Includes excellent supporting details. Shows creativity; uses a distinctive voice.	Purpose is clear and presented in an organized, engaging way. Includes relevant supporting details.	Purpose or argument is vague. Organization is weak or inconsistent.	Topic is unclear. There are few supporting details and little evidence of organization.
Critical reading/ responding to literature		Provides excellent summaries in response to prompts. Pays close attention to detail and context, and makes valid inferences about the author's meaning, purpose, or point of view when asked.	Summarizes ideas and themes adequately in response to prompts. Pays attention to details and context. Questions and inferences reflect a good understanding of the author's purpose or point of view.	Can summarize action or characters, but struggles to summarize ideas and themes. Identifies details and context, but has difficulty interpreting information or drawing conclusions.	Cannot summarize ideas or themes. Little or no attention to detail or context. Contributes little or nothing to discussion.
Responses to peers' comments		Contributes insightful remarks that add value to the original post and encourage ongoing online discussion by asking a question, extending an idea, or offering a differing point of view.	Contributes remarks that add some value to the original post by asking a question, extending an idea, or offering a differing point of view.	Contributes remarks, but adds little value to the original post because these remarks are limited to expressing agreement with the original author's point of view.	Contributes little in the way of remarks and those posted show little or no insight related to the topic.
Final product		Meets all criteria for activity. Written contributions exceed expectations and reflect excellent understanding of activity content.	Meets all activity criteria. Written contributions meet expectations and reflect good understanding of activity content.	Meets most activity criteria. Some elements or components are missing.	Did not contribute to the online environment; either did not post work or is missing major components.
Presentation		Completed within specific time. Evidence of preparation is obvious. Emphasizes most important information. All team members are involved.	Almost completed within time. Some preparation evident. Covers majority of main points. Not all team members involved.	Almost completed within time. Little preparation evident. Misses a number of important points. Not all team members involved.	Did not participate, did not prepare; is way under or over time, or information is confusing and disjointed.
Teamwork		Workload divided and shared equally by all members.	Most members, including student, contributed fair share.	Workloads varied considerably. Student did not contribute fair share.	Few members contributed. Student made little or no contribution.
Class participation		Contributed substantially.	Contributed fair share.	Contributed some.	Contributed very little.

1 WORKING IN A WIKI

Instructional Objectives

Students will be able to:

- Log in to a class wiki and edit a wiki page.

- Insert an image on a wiki page.

- Add a comment or discussion remark on a wiki page.

Time frame: one class period

Structure: whole class and individual

IRA/NCTE Standard

Standard 8—Students use a variety of technological and information resources (e.g., libraries, databases, computer networks, video) to gather and synthesize information and to create and communicate knowledge.

NETS*S Standard

Standard 6. Technology Operations and Concepts—Students demonstrate a sound understanding of technology concepts, systems, and operations.

Framework for 21st Century Learning

ICT Literacy—Use technology as a tool to research, organize, evaluate and communicate information.

Materials/Hardware/Software

- Student Activity Page (one copy per student)

- Classroom wiki
  Wiki hosts frequently used by educators include PBWorks (http://pbworks.com), Wikispaces (www.wikispaces.com), and Wetpaint (www.wetpaint.com). Each host offers an ad-free option for educators, but you need to follow the directions provided carefully to get a no-cost, ad-free education wiki.

- Digital image (for students to use when practicing how to insert an image)

- One Internet-connected desktop or laptop computer per student

Teacher Preparation

Prior to teaching this lesson, you need to do the following:

1. Set up a classroom wiki.

2. Depending upon the wiki host you select, either set a password for students to use when editing pages or create individual wiki host accounts for student use when editing. Provide this information to students prior to beginning this lesson. It may save time to have your students set up their own individual accounts at the beginning of this lesson. Consult your district's Acceptable Use Policy to see if this is permissible.

3. Add the URL for the wiki to the Student Activity Page before duplicating that page.

4. Create a wiki page called Practice Pages and link this page to the wiki's front or main page.

5. Create an individual practice page for each student. Each page must have a unique name, such as Activity 1, Activity 2, etc. Link these pages to the wiki page called Practice Pages and assign a page to each student. Provide the page assignments prior to starting this lesson. If you are teaching this lesson to multiple class periods, you may want to group these page lists by period.

6. Upload a digital photo into the wiki file storage area. Students will use this photo as part of the activity. If you do not have a digital image, go to Flickr (http://flickr.com), where you will be able to search the Creative Commons area to find an appropriate image to upload to the wiki. Be sure to read the directions for inserting an image on a page, which you will find in the wiki's Help section.

7. Check to be sure that each student has a current, signed Acceptable Use Policy on file.

8. Arrange for students to have one-to-one access to Internet-connected desktop or laptop computers for this activity. This may require scheduling lab time or borrowing a laptop cart.

Prerequisite Student Skills

Students need to know how to:

1. Open a Web browser

2. Enter a URL in the address bar and navigate to a Web site

3. Find a specified link in a wiki sidebar or navigation bar

4. Log in to the class wiki site

Vocabulary

wiki: a Web site where multiple users can create, modify, and delete content found on the site regardless of who originally wrote and posted the material

wiki host: an online service that provides an application subscribers use to create their own wikis. The host also stores the wiki on a server for ongoing access. Although each wiki application may have a few unique features, nearly all wiki applications offer the same basic capabilities for creating and editing wiki pages.

Teaching Tips

- Wikis permit just one person to edit a page at a time. However, all your students can be working simultaneously if they have an individual page to edit. This is why it saves time and helps with classroom management if you create individual practice pages before the lesson. Once these pages are created, students can use them for this type of practice activity throughout the school year.

- Go through this activity yourself before assigning it to students. This will help you anticipate problems that might arise.

Activities/Procedures

1. **Accessing the Wiki**—Distribute the Student Activity Page. Ask students to open the Web browser and use the wiki URL written on the activity sheet to navigate to the wiki. Students should already have the practice page assignment and log-in information. If having students create their own individual wiki accounts, do that now. (approximately 5–10 minutes)

2. **Adding and Formatting Text**—Once each student accesses his or her individual practice page, he or she enters the text provided on the Student Activity Page and experiments with formatting tools. (approximately 15 minutes)

3. **Inserting an Image**—Walk the class through this portion of the activity to show them where the image file is stored and how to insert the image file into their individual wiki practice pages. (approximately 10 minutes)

4. **Adding a Comment**—Review the directions with the class and allow students to add their comments or discussion remarks to the Practice Pages page. (approximately 10 minutes)

Assessment/Evaluation

- Monitor students while they are working.

- Check student practice pages to see if students successfully added and formatted text and an image.

- Check the main Practice Pages page to review student comments posted on that page.

Follow-up Activities

- Literary Analysis—21st Century Style
- Build Your Own Reference Library—Glossary of Terms
- Build Your Own Reference Library—Formatting and Style Guide
- Read All About It

Meeting the Needs of Diverse Learners

You might find that students with different abilities will benefit from extra help or extra challenges.

- Students who need extra help will benefit from working through this activity with a partner. Also, because the wiki is online, these students can continue to practice these skills anywhere they have access to the Internet.

- Students who would benefit from extra challenges can explore an existing wiki such as Wikipedia (www.wikipedia.org) to see how pages are set up, conventions for editing, and so on. These students could also create suggested class norms for editing or commenting on classmates' work.

Recommended Internet Sites

- PBWorks (http://pbworks.com)
- Wikispaces (www.wikispaces.com)
- Wetpaint (www.wetpaint.com)
- Wikipedia (www.wikipedia.org)
- Flickr (http://flickr.com)

Answer Key

There are no right or wrong answers for this activity. Check student practice pages to see if students successfully added and formatted text and an image. Check the main Practice Pages page to review student comments posted on that page.

1 WORKING IN A WIKI

Objective

During this activity, you will log in to a class wiki, edit a wiki page, insert an image on a wiki page, and add a comment or discussion remark on a wiki page.

Before You Begin

A wiki is a Web site where multiple users can create, modify, and delete content found on the site. Users can do this regardless of who originally wrote and posted the material. You've probably heard about or used Wikipedia. It is a popular online general reference site. Did you realize that you can use a wiki for your own schoolwork? The purpose of this activity is to ensure that you have the basic technology skills needed to use a classroom wiki for team and individual work.

Materials

- Student Activity Page
- Wiki URL: _____
- Log-in information (either assigned by your teacher or created by you when you first access the wiki page): _____
- Wiki Practice Pages name (provided by teacher): _____

Directions

Accessing the Wiki

1. Open the computer's Web browser. Use the wiki URL provided above to get to the classroom wiki.

2. Log in to the wiki. You may need to follow the directions your teacher provides to set up an individual wiki account to use for all wiki assignments.

3. Click on the **Practice Pages** link on the wiki's main page.

4. Find the wiki practice page assigned to you and click on that link.

Adding and Formatting Text

1. Wiki pages can be viewed in two different ways: as a regular Web page or as a document that can be edited. To view your practice page in Edit mode, click the button or tab labeled **Edit.** The wiki page should now look just like a word processing document, including a formatting toolbar that looks similar to this:

2. Type the following text on your practice page:

   To enter text, I place the cursor over the text box, click one time, and begin to type.

   When I'm done typing, I need to click on the Save button or tab.

   To add more text or to format existing text, I just need to click on the button or tab labeled Edit and I can make changes. Once again, I need to click Save to keep the changes.

3. **Save** the text you just typed.

4. Click **Edit** to go back into Edit mode.

5. Experiment with some of the formatting tools. For example, make a word **bold**, or *italic.* Change the font or the font size. Change the text color.

6. **Save** the formatting you have added.

Inserting an Image

Every wiki host allows users to add images to pages. Most often you:

1. Upload a photo into the wiki's file storage area.

2. Go into **Edit** mode on the wiki page where you want to add the photo.

3. Place the cursor where you want the photo to appear.

4. Click the **Insert image** tool in the formatting toolbar.

5. Follow the directions that appear on the screen.

Follow the directions your teacher gives now to insert an image on your wiki practice page.

Adding a Comment

Wiki hosts encourage communication among users. This is done through **Discussion** or **Comment** features. This will be useful when you and your classmates use the class wiki for assignments. Comments are not anonymous. You must be logged in to post a comment or join a discussion. The final activity in this lesson is to post a comment or discussion remark on the **Practice Pages** page where you located the link to your individual practice page.

1. Make sure you are logged in to the wiki.

2. Navigate to the **Practice Pages** page of the wiki.

3. Find and click on the button or tab labeled **Discussions**. Or, scroll to the bottom of the wiki page to find a text box marked **Comment**.

4. Write a one-sentence comment about what you have learned in this activity.

5. Post the comment. Remember, comments are not anonymous, so think about what you write.

2 LITERARY ANALYSIS—21ST CENTURY STYLE

Instructional Objectives

Students will be able to:

- Work in a small group to contribute to a class analysis of a work of fiction.

- Log in to and edit pages of a class wiki.

- Add comments or discussion remarks on a wiki page.

Time frame: one class period

Structure: groups of 3–4 students

IRA/NCTE Standards

Standard 3—Students apply a wide range of strategies to comprehend, interpret, evaluate, and appreciate texts. They draw on their prior experience, their interactions with other readers and writers, their knowledge of word meaning and of other texts, their word identification strategies, and their understanding of textual features (e.g., sound-letter correspondence, sentence structure, context, graphics).

Standard 8—Students use a variety of technological and information resources (e.g., libraries, databases, computer networks, video) to gather and synthesize information and to create and communicate knowledge.

NETS*S Standards

Standard 4. Critical Thinking, Problem Solving, and Decision Making—Students use critical thinking skills to plan and conduct research, manage projects, solve problems, and make informed decisions using appropriate digital tools and resources.

Standard 6. Technology Operations and Concepts—Students demonstrate a sound understanding of technology concepts, systems, and operations.

Framework for 21st Century Learning

Core Subjects and 21st Century Themes—Mastery of core subjects and 21st century themes is essential for students in the 21st century.

ICT Literacy—Use technology as a tool to research, organize, evaluate and communicate information.

Materials/Hardware/Software

- Student Activity Page (one copy per student)

- Team pages on a classroom wiki for students to use as they contribute to a class analysis of a work of fiction

- If you need to set up a wiki, refer to the Teacher Preparation section of Lesson 1, Working in a Wiki.

- Language Arts textbooks, dictionaries, or other reference sources that include definitions for terms related to literary analysis

- Scratch paper for brainstorming

- One Internet-connected desktop or laptop computer per student team

Teacher Preparation

Prior to teaching this lesson, you need to do the following:

1. Decide which elements of a literary work you want students to analyze (e.g., plot, characters, point of view, setting, symbols).

2. Create teams of 3–4 students and assign one element of the analysis to each team. For example, with ten teams, you might have one team work on setting, two teams work on characters (antagonist and protagonist), one team work on symbols, one team work on point of view, and five teams work on different elements of plot (exposition, rising action, climax, falling action, and resolution).

3. Create a new page for your classroom wiki and make its title the literary work your students will analyze. Link this page to the wiki's front or main page. (If you need to set up a wiki, refer to the Teacher Preparation section of Lesson 1, Working in a Wiki.)

4. Create a working wiki page for each team. Use the name of the literary work and the element of the analysis that team will work on as the title for the page. Link the team pages to the title page you created for this activity.

5. Add a general prompt to each page, such as: "Your team is analyzing the (fill in the blank) for this literary work. Begin by adding a definition for this element of literary analysis. Next, describe or identify the (fill in the blank) and explain how the (fill in the blank) contributes to the reader's understanding of the literary work." Make this prompt as specific as you want.

6. Add the URL for the wiki to the Student Activity Page before duplicating that page.

7. Provide the students' team assignments prior to starting this lesson.

8. Arrange for each team of students to have access to one Internet-connected desktop or laptop computer for this activity. This may require scheduling lab time or borrowing a laptop cart.

Prerequisite Student Skills

Students need to be familiar with:

1. How to log in to the class wiki site, add and edit text, and comment on wiki pages

2. The various elements of a piece of fiction that can be analyzed to learn more about the work

Vocabulary

literary analysis: the act of separating a work of fiction into its parts (e.g., plot, characters, point of view, symbols) to gain a better understanding of the whole

wiki: a Web site where multiple users can create, modify, and delete content found on the site regardless of who originally wrote and posted the material

Teaching Tip

Because wikis permit just one person to edit a page at a time, student teams will need to identify a typist and work together to add text to their assigned page. Once the initial work is done, students may access the wiki from any Internet-connected computer to make additions, edits, or comments.

Activities/Procedures

1. **Accessing the Wiki**—Distribute the Student Activity Page. Ask students to open the Web browser and use the wiki URL written on the activity sheet to navigate to the wiki. Team members should already know how to log in to work on the wiki; they should also know which element of the analysis they have been assigned. (approximately 5 minutes)

2. **Writing a Definition of the Element**—To ensure that students understand the element of analysis they are assigned, give them a few minutes to write a definition for this element and add it to the wiki page. Encourage students to use print or online sources for the definition. (approximately 10 minutes)

3. **Discussing Ideas and Adding Text to the Wiki Page**—Teams brainstorm ideas about the element of analysis they are working on and come to an agreement on the text they will add to the wiki page. (approximately 30 minutes)

4. **Adding a Comment**—Give teams a few minutes to review another team's work and add a comment or discussion remark to that wiki page. (approximately 5 minutes)

Assessment/Evaluation

- Monitor students while they are working.

- Check team pages to see if students accurately defined the element of analysis their team was assigned.

- Check team pages to see if students successfully identified or described the element of analysis their team worked on and if they were able to accurately explain how this element impacts the reader's understanding of the literary work.

Follow-up Activities

- This analysis can become a living document. Encourage students to refer back to and edit or comment on these wiki pages whenever appropriate.

- Use the class wiki to analyze a variety of different literary works.

- Encourage students to use comments or discussion remarks to interact with one another and engage in deeper conversations about various elements of the analysis.

Meeting the Needs of Diverse Learners

You might find that students with different abilities will benefit from extra help or extra challenges.

- When setting up the teams, think about creating groups in which students' strengths will complement one another, and provide support to students who might need extra help.

- Students who would benefit from extra challenges can review and comment on the work done by other teams. You might also challenge them to discover how to receive automated notifications whenever a new comment is posted. Remind these students that this is an opportunity for them to model norms for discussing other students' work.

Recommended Internet Sites

- Merriam-Webster Online (www.merriam-webster.com)

- Dictionary.com (http://dictionary.reference.com)

Answer Key

Answers will vary depending upon the literary work chosen and the elements analyzed. Accept all reasonable responses.

2 LITERARY ANALYSIS—21ST CENTURY STYLE

Objective

During this activity, you will work in a small group to analyze a work of fiction using the class wiki.

Before You Begin

When reading a play, short story, or novel, it's important to analyze the different parts of the work. For example, you might think about the setting, the characters, and the elements of the plot. Using a wiki, it's possible for you to work with a team to write an analysis with your entire class. And once the analysis is done, you can still use the wiki pages as a reference or model for other assignments.

You will complete this activity with two or three classmates (as assigned by your teacher).

Materials

- Student Activity Page

- Wiki URL: _____

- Team analysis topic (provided by your teacher): _____

- Language Arts textbook, dictionary, or other reference source that defines terms related to literary analysis

- Scratch paper for brainstorming

Directions

Accessing the Wiki

1. Open the computer's Web browser.

2. Use the wiki URL provided above to get to the classroom wiki for this activity.

3. Look at the links on this main wiki page. Find your team's link. Your teacher has assigned one element of the literary analysis to your team.

4. Click to open your team working page.

Write a Definition of the Element

1. Before beginning your analysis, work with your team members to define the element you will work with.

2. Find a definition for the element your team is assigned (e.g., setting, protagonist, or plot climax). Use your textbook, a dictionary (online or off-line), or other reference book to do this.

3. Discuss the definition. Be sure all team members agree on its meaning.

4. Choose a typist. Have that person type the definition on your team's wiki page.

5. Click **Save**.

Discuss Ideas and Add Text to the Wiki Page

1. Take about five minutes to brainstorm ideas about the element you are analyzing.

2. Use a piece of paper to jot down your ideas.

3. Describe or identify the element (e.g., who is the protagonist or what is the setting).

4. Next, explain how this element contributes to the reader's understanding of the literary work.

5. As a team, come to an agreement on your answers.

6. Have the typist add this information to the wiki page.

7. Take a few minutes to proofread your work and make edits or additions.

8. Click **Save**.

Adding a Comment

If there is time, view other teams' pages. If you have a question or comment, use the **Discussion** or **Comment** feature on the wiki page to make your remark. Remember, comments are not anonymous, so think about what you write.

3 BUILD YOUR OWN REFERENCE LIBRARY— GLOSSARY OF TERMS

Instructional Objectives

Students will be able to:

- Contribute to an online glossary of terms.

- Peer edit definitions and examples written by classmates.

Time frame: 20 minutes

Structure: groups of 3–4 students

IRA/NCTE Standards

Standard 3—Students apply a wide range of strategies to comprehend, interpret, evaluate, and appreciate texts. They draw on their prior experience, their interactions with other readers and writers, their knowledge of word meaning and of other texts, their word identification strategies, and their understanding of textual features (e.g., sound-letter correspondence, sentence structure, context, graphics).

Standard 8—Students use a variety of technological and information resources (e.g., libraries, databases, computer networks, video) to gather and synthesize information and to create and communicate knowledge.

NETS*S Standards

Standard 2. Communication and Collaboration—Students use digital media and environments to communicate and work collaboratively, including at a distance, to support individual learning and contribute to the learning of others.

Standard 3. Research and Information Fluency—Students apply digital tools to gather, evaluate, and use information.

Framework for 21st Century Learning

Communication and Collaboration—Assume shared responsibility for collaborative work, and value the individual contributions made by each team member.

Information Literacy—Access and evaluate information.

Materials/Hardware/Software

- Student Activity Page (one copy per student)
- Team pages on a classroom wiki for students to use as they contribute to a class glossary of terms (If you need to set up a wiki, refer to the Teacher Preparation section of Lesson 1, Working in a Wiki.)
- Language Arts textbooks, dictionaries, or other reference sources that include definitions for glossary terms
- Notebook paper for drafting the definition and an example
- One Internet-connected desktop or laptop computer per student team

Teacher Preparation

Prior to teaching this lesson, you need to do the following:

1. Decide how the glossary will be structured. You might have terms grouped by instructional unit or in alphabetical order. Remember that you need to use a structure that allows, at least at first, several teams of students to each have a page to work on at the same time. Once students are comfortable with working on the glossary, you can assign additions and edits as homework.

2. Create teams of 3–4 students and assign one glossary term to each team. For example, with five teams, you might divide the alphabet into five groups and have each team add a term, definition, and example to one of the wiki pages for that letter group.

3. Create a new page for your classroom wiki and title it Glossary of Terms. Link this page to the wiki's front or main page. (If you need to set up a wiki, refer to the Teacher Preparation section of Lesson 1, Working in a Wiki.)

4. Create a working wiki page for each section of the glossary. (Initially you'll want to have enough pages so each team can easily add a term and definition. Later you might combine pages.) Use the name of the subcategories you have chosen as the title for each working page (e.g., A–E, F–J). Link the working pages to the title page you created for the glossary.

5. Add a statement to the main glossary page to explain its purpose. You may or may not need a prompt on each of the remaining glossary pages, depending on how the glossary is organized. For instance, if the glossary is alphabetical, you may simply want to remind students to add new terms in alphabetical order and then add letter headings.

6. Add the URL for the main glossary page to the Student Activity Page before duplicating that page.

7. Provide the students' team assignments prior to starting this lesson.

8. Arrange for each team of students to have access to one Internet-connected desktop or laptop computer for this activity. This may require scheduling lab time or borrowing a laptop cart.

Prerequisite Student Skills

Students need to be familiar with:

1. How to log in to the class wiki site and add and edit text

2. Reference materials they can use to find definitions for the glossary

Vocabulary

glossary: a list of terms and their definitions related to a specific topic or area of knowledge; a glossary may also include examples of how or when a term is used

wiki: a Web site that allows multiple users to create, modify, and delete content found on the site regardless of who originally wrote and posted the material

Teaching Tip

Initially, student teams will need to identify a typist and work together to add terms, definitions, and examples to their assigned page. Once students know how to add terms to the glossary, they may access the wiki from any Internet-connected computer to make ongoing additions, edits, or comments.

Activities/Procedures

1. **Accessing the Wiki**—Distribute the Student Activity Page. Ask students to open the Web browser and use the wiki URL written on the activity sheet to navigate to the wiki. Team members should already know how to log in to work on the wiki; they should also know which glossary page they have been assigned for this activity. (approximately 5 minutes)

2. **Navigating the Glossary**—Provide a brief overview of the glossary. Be sure students understand that they are to add a term, a definition, and an example on the page they have been assigned for this activity. (approximately 5 minutes)

3. **Adding a Glossary Entry**—Each team identifies a typist who adds their assigned term in the appropriate location on the glossary page. Team members then research definitions for their term, discuss their findings, and write a definition and example that will be added to the glossary. The typist adds the term, definition, and example to the wiki page. (approximately 10 minutes)

Assessment/Evaluation

- Monitor students while they are working.

- Check glossary pages to see if students accurately defined the term their team was assigned and provided an example.

- Check glossary pages for follow-up edits and/or comments.

Follow-up Activities

- This glossary can be used throughout the school year. Have students add terms, refer back to, and edit or comment on these wiki pages whenever appropriate.

- Encourage students to use comments or discussion remarks to interact with one another and engage in peer review of the glossary entries.

Meeting the Needs of Diverse Learners

You might find that students with different abilities will benefit from extra help or extra challenges.

- When forming teams, think about creating groups in which students' strengths will complement one another, and provide support to students who might need extra help.

- Students who would benefit from extra challenges can use digital cameras to take photos that illustrate various terms, and then upload and insert the photos on glossary pages.

Recommended Internet Sites

- Merriam-Webster Online (www.merriam-webster.com)

- Dictionary.com (http://dictionary.reference.com)

Answer Key

Answers will vary depending upon the terms chosen. Accept all reasonable definitions and examples.

3 BUILD YOUR OWN REFERENCE LIBRARY— GLOSSARY OF TERMS

Objective

During this activity, you will work in a small group to contribute to a class glossary of terms using the class wiki.

Before You Begin

The ability to understand and use new words is a lifelong skill. Until very recently, you probably learned vocabulary by copying a list of words, looking up definitions, and keeping the list in a notebook. Today, you can work with other students to create a glossary of terms using a wiki. In this activity, you will work in a small group to learn how to add entries to an online glossary of terms. Your class will use the glossary throughout the school year.

Materials

- Student Activity Page
- URL for Glossary of Terms wiki page: _____
- Glossary term your team will add (provided by your teacher): _____
- Notebook paper for drafting the definition and an example
- Language Arts textbook, dictionary, or other reference sources that your team can use to find term definitions

Directions

Accessing the Wiki

1. Open the computer's Web browser.

2. Use the wiki URL written on the activity sheet to get to the main glossary page in the wiki.

3. Get the term your teacher has assigned and your glossary page needed to complete this activity.

Navigating the Glossary

1. Listen as your teacher provides a brief overview of the glossary.

2. Be sure you understand how to add a term, a definition, and an example on the page your team has been assigned for this activity.

3. If necessary, ask clarifying questions.

Adding a Glossary Entry

1. Identify a team typist. This person needs to type your assigned term in the appropriate location on the glossary page.

2. As a team, research definitions for this term and discuss your findings.

3. On a sheet of paper, write a definition. Come up with an example that will be added to the glossary. Be sure all team members agree on the definition and the example.

4. When you are ready, have the typist add the term, definition, and example to the wiki page.

BUILD YOUR OWN REFERENCE LIBRARY—FORMATTING AND STYLE GUIDE

Instructional Objectives

Students will be able to:

- Contribute to an online formatting and style guide.

- Peer edit entries and examples written by classmates.

Time frame: 20 minutes

Structure: groups of 3–4 students

IRA/NCTE Standards

Standard 4—Students adjust their use of spoken, written, and visual language (e.g., conventions, style, vocabulary) to communicate effectively with a variety of audiences and for different purposes.

Standard 8—Students use a variety of technological and information resources (e.g., libraries, databases, computer networks, video) to gather and synthesize information and to create and communicate knowledge.

NETS*S Standards

Standard 2. Communication and Collaboration—Students use digital media and environments to communicate and work collaboratively, including at a distance, to support individual learning and contribute to the learning of others.

Standard 3. Research and Information Fluency—Students apply digital tools to gather, evaluate, and use information.

Framework for 21st Century Learning

Communication and Collaboration—Assume shared responsibility for collaborative work, and value the individual contributions made by each team member.

Information Literacy—Access and evaluate information.

Materials/Hardware/Software

- Student Activity Page (one copy per student)

- Team pages on a classroom wiki for students to use as they contribute to a class style guide (If you need to set up a wiki, refer to the Teacher Preparation section of Lesson 1, Working in a Wiki.)

- Style guides, style manuals, and other reference materials students can use to identify appropriate entries and examples for the online style guide

- Notebook paper for drafting the entry and an example

- One Internet-connected desktop or laptop computer per student team

Teacher Preparation

Prior to teaching this lesson, you need to do the following:

1. Decide how the formatting and style guide will be structured. You will probably want to use some kind of organizational format in which entries are grouped by type (e.g., footnotes, abbreviations, bibliographic citations). Remember that you need to use a structure such that, at least at first, several teams of students each have a page to work on at the same time. Once students are comfortable with working on the formatting and style guide, you can assign additions and edits as homework.

2. Create teams of 3–4 students and assign one entry and example to each team. For example, with five teams, you might have five different topic pages in the wiki on which each team can add one entry and example during this introductory activity.

3. Create a new page for your classroom wiki and title it Formatting and Style Guide. Link this page to the wiki's front or main page. (If you need to set up a wiki, refer to the Teacher Preparation section of Lesson 1, Working in a Wiki.)

4. Create a working wiki page for each section of the formatting and style guide. (Initially you'll want to have enough pages so each team can easily add a term and definition. Later you will probably need to create additional pages.) Use the name of the subcategories you have chosen as the title for each working page (e.g., Footnotes, Abbreviations, Bibliographic Citations). Link the working pages to the title page you created for the formatting and style guide.

5. Add a statement to the main formatting and style guide page to explain its purpose. You may or may not need a prompt on each of the remaining pages, depending on how the formatting and style guide is organized.

6. Add the URL for the main formatting and style guide page to the Student Activity Page before duplicating that page.

7. Give students their team assignments prior to beginning the lesson.

8. Arrange for each team of students to have access to one Internet-connected desktop or laptop computer for this activity. This may require scheduling lab time or borrowing a laptop cart.

Prerequisite Student Skills

Students need to be familiar with:

1. How to log in to the class wiki site and add and edit text

2. Reference materials they can use to find entries for the formatting and style guide

Vocabulary

formatting and style guide: a set of rules or guidelines for designing and writing documents, often specific to a school or institution

wiki: a Web site that allows multiple users to create, modify, and delete content found on the site regardless of who originally wrote and posted the material

Teaching Tip

Check to see if your school already has a formatting and style guide. If so, you may want to have students add this information to the online guide, along with updates and new entries for items not covered in the school's existing guide. Once students know how to add entries and examples to the guide, they may access the wiki from any Internet-connected computer to make ongoing additions, edits, or comments.

Activities/Procedures

1. **Accessing the Wiki**—Distribute the Student Activity Page. Ask students to open the Web browser and use the wiki URL written on the activity sheet to navigate to the wiki. Team members should already know how to log in to work on the wiki; they should also know which formatting and style guide page they have been assigned for this activity. (approximately 5 minutes)

2. **Navigating the Formatting and Style Guide**—Provide a brief overview of the online guide. Be sure students understand that they are to add an entry and an example on the page they have been assigned for this activity. (approximately 5 minutes)

3. **Adding a Guide Entry**—Team members research their entry, discuss their findings, and write text and an example that will be added to the guide. The team then chooses a typist who adds the entry and example to the wiki page. (approximately 10 minutes)

Assessment/Evaluation

- Monitor students while they are working.

- Check guide pages to see if the entries and examples written by the students are accurate.

- Check guide pages for follow-up edits and/or comments.

Follow-up Activities

- This formatting and style guide can be used throughout the school year. Have students write additional entries, refer back to, and edit or comment on these wiki pages whenever appropriate.

- Encourage students to use comments or discussion remarks to interact with one another and engage in peer review of the formatting and style entries.

Meeting the Needs of Diverse Learners

You might find that students with different abilities will benefit from extra help or extra challenges.

- Consider having students who need extra help work on paper before entering the information on the wiki.

- Students who would benefit from extra challenges can use their experience with this online guide to set up wiki pages for a class grammar guide.

Recommended Internet Sites

- APA Formatting and Style Guide (http://owl.english.purdue.edu/owl/resource/560/01/)

- MLA Formatting and Style Guide (http://owl.english.purdue.edu/owl/resource/557/01/)

- College and university online style guides: Writing (Editorial) Style Guides (www.wmich.edu/wmu/writing/others/index.html)

Answer Key

Answers will vary depending upon the assigned entries. Accept all reasonable entries and examples.

4 BUILD YOUR OWN REFERENCE LIBRARY— FORMATTING AND STYLE GUIDE

Objective

During this activity, you will work in a small group to contribute to a class formatting and style guide using the class wiki.

Before You Begin

Most schools and many businesses set their own rules for designing and writing documents. These standards are often based on style formats such as MLA (written by the Modern Language Association of America) or APA (from the American Psychological Association). They can be based on more than one format, too. It's important for you to be aware of style guides. Written schoolwork that does not follow these rules might be given a lower grade or not be graded at all. And, in the business world, written materials that do not conform to these rules might be set aside without ever being read.

Your class will create a formatting and style guide using the class wiki. You will work in a small group to learn how to add entries to the formatting and style guide. Your class can use this guide throughout the school year.

Materials

- Student Activity Page
- URL for main formatting and style guide wiki page:

  _____

- Title of entry your team will add (provided by your teacher):

  _____

- Style guides, style manuals, and other reference materials that your team can use to identify appropriate entries and examples for the online style guide
- Notebook paper for drafting the entry and an example

Directions

Accessing the Wiki

1. Open the Web browser.

2. Use the wiki URL written on this activity sheet to get to the main formatting and style guide page in the wiki.

3. Go to the assigned wiki page for your team to use to complete this activity.

Navigating the Formatting and Style Guide

1. Follow along as your teacher provides a brief overview of the formatting and style guide.

2. Be sure you understand how to add an entry and example on the page your team has been assigned for this activity.

3. If necessary, ask clarifying questions.

Adding a Guide Entry

1. As a team, research your assigned entry topic.

2. Discuss your findings.

3. Write an entry on a sheet of paper. Include an example that will be added to the guide. Be sure all team members agree on the wording of the entry and the example.

4. When you are ready, choose a team typist. The typist then adds the entry and example to the wiki page.

Here is a sample:

Paper Headings
Do not use a title page unless your teacher tells you to include one. A proper heading is placed in the upper left-hand corner of the first page. It includes the student's name, the teacher's name, the class period, and the date. When typed, this information is double-spaced.

Example:

Jane Doe

Mr. John Garcia

Period 3

May 31, 2012

READ ALL ABOUT IT

Instructional Objectives

Students will be able to:

- Contribute to an online collection of book reviews.

- Comment on reviews written by classmates.

Time frame: 45–50 minutes

Structure: individual

IRA/NCTE Standards

Standard 8—Students use a variety of technological and information resources (e.g., libraries, databases, computer networks, video) to gather and synthesize information and to create and communicate knowledge.

Standard 12—Students use spoken, written, and visual language to accomplish their own purposes (e.g., for learning, enjoyment, persuasion, and the exchange of information).

NETS*S Standard

Standard 2. Communication and Collaboration—Students use digital media and environments to communicate and work collaboratively, including at a distance, to support individual learning and contribute to the learning of others.

Framework for 21st Century Learning

Communication and Collaboration—Articulate thoughts and ideas effectively using oral, written and nonverbal communication skills in a variety of forms and contexts.

Communication and Collaboration—Use communication for a range of purposes (e.g., to inform, instruct, motivate, and persuade).

Materials/Hardware/Software

- Student Activity Page (one copy per student)

- Individual practice page for each student linked to a main Practice Pages page (If your students completed Lesson 1, Working in a Wiki, they already have an individual practice page. If not, please refer to the Teacher Preparation section of that lesson to see how to set up individual practice pages.)

- One copy of a book read by the student per student

- One Internet-connected desktop or laptop computer per student

Teacher Preparation

Prior to teaching this lesson, you need to do the following:

1. Decide how the book review section will be structured. Consider organizing reviews by genre (e.g., mystery, historical fiction, biography) or similar grouping. Students will write the first review on their individual practice pages. Students will later copy their reviews and paste them onto the correct book review page. Students will add future reviews directly to the appropriate book review page.

2. Make sure each student has a copy of a book he or she has read and can review.

3. Create a new page for your classroom wiki and title it Book Reviews. Link this page to the wiki's front or main page. (If you need to set up a wiki, refer to the Teacher Preparation section of Lesson 1, Working in a Wiki.)

4. Create a working wiki page for each section of Book Reviews. For example, begin with a page about a genre studied in class. Add pages as needed. Use the name of each genre selected as the title for each working page, (e.g., Mystery, Historical Fiction, Biography).

5. Link the working pages to the title page you created for Book Reviews.

6. Add a statement to the main Book Reviews page to explain its purpose. You may or may not need a prompt on each of the genre pages, depending upon how well the students follow the review format established in this activity.

7. Add the URL for the main Book Reviews page to the Student Activity Page before duplicating that page.

8. Arrange for each student to have access to an Internet-connected desktop or laptop computer for this activity. This may require scheduling lab time or borrowing a laptop cart.

Prerequisite Student Skills

Students need to:

1. Know how to log in to the class wiki site and add and edit text

2. Know how to make comments or post discussion remarks on a wiki page

3. Read a book that can be reviewed for this activity

Vocabulary

book review: a short summary and evaluation of a book

wiki: a Web site that allows multiple users to create, modify, and delete content found on the site regardless of who originally wrote and posted the material

Teaching Tip

If your school has a library/media specialist, he or she might already have a book review system in place that you can use with your students. If not, he or she might be interested in collaborating on this activity with you. Once students understand how to write a review and make comments about other reviews, this area of the wiki can be an ongoing option for student book reports.

Activities/Procedures

1. **Accessing the Wiki**—Distribute the Student Activity Page. Ask students to open the Web browser and use the wiki URL written on the activity sheet to navigate to the wiki. Students should already have the practice page assignment and log-in information. (approximately 5 minutes)

2. **Navigating the Book Reviews Section**—Provide a brief overview of the Book Reviews section. Be sure students understand that they are to copy and paste their individual reviews onto the group page later. (approximately 10 minutes)

3. **Writing a Book Review**—Students write a summary of the book they are reviewing and an evaluation of the book on individual practice pages. (approximately 20 minutes)

4. **Posting the Book Review**—Group the students by genre and have them take turns copying and pasting their reviews onto the assigned page. While waiting their turn, students may read and comment on other reviews that have already been posted. (approximately 10 minutes)

Assessment/Evaluation

- Monitor students while they are working.

- Check reviews to see if they include a summary and evaluation.

- Check book review pages for follow-up edits and/or comments.

Follow-up Activities

- This book review section can be used throughout the school year. Have students write additional reviews for, refer back to, and edit or comment on these wiki pages whenever appropriate.

- Encourage students to use comments or discussion remarks to interact with one another and engage in discussions about the books.

Meeting the Needs of Diverse Learners

You might find that students with different abilities will benefit from extra help or extra challenges.

- Students who need extra help will benefit from reading with a buddy and then working with that student to write and post a joint review.

- Students who would benefit from extra challenges can peer edit other students' reviews or help with moving initial reviews from practice pages into the book review section of the wiki.

Recommended Internet Sites

- How to Write a Book Review (www.pwcs.edu/schools/es/pattie/archive-pattie/ summer%20reading/howtodoabookreview.htm)

- How to Write a Book Report (www.infoplease.com/homework/wsbookreporths.html)

Answer Key

Answers will vary depending upon the books reviewed. Accept all reasonable responses.

5 **READ ALL ABOUT IT**

Objective

During this activity, you will add to an online set of book reviews. You will also comment on at least one review written by another student.

Before You Begin

You have probably read and then written reports about books. One purpose of the report is to ensure you have actually read the book. Another far more interesting purpose is to share information with other readers. In this activity, you and your classmates will be writing reviews of books and making book recommendations to each other. You will post these reviews in a new section of the class wiki called "Book Reviews." In addition, you will read and comment on reviews written by your classmates.

Your class will use this section of the class wiki throughout the school year.

Materials

- Student Activity Page
- URL for main wiki page: _____
- Copy of a book you have read

Directions

Accessing the Wiki

1. Open the Web browser. Use the wiki URL written on this activity sheet to get to the main page of the class wiki.

2. Click on the **Practice Pages** link on the wiki's main page.

3. Find the wiki practice page assigned to you. Click on that link. *This is the same practice page you used in the Working in a Wiki activity.*

Navigating the Book Reviews Section

1. Listen as your teacher explains the Book Reviews section of the wiki.

2. Be sure you know how to find the genre page. This is where you will paste your finished book review.

3. Draft a book review. Post it on your practice page.

4. If necessary, ask clarifying questions.

Writing a Book Review

Your book review needs to contain certain basic information no matter what genre the book falls into. Here is a sample outline:

Title of book:

Author:

Illustrator (if appropriate):

Number of pages:

Summary

Use this section of the review to describe the book.

- What is the setting?

- Who are the main characters?

- What is the conflict?

Do not give away the end of the book!

Evaluation

Use this portion of the review to discuss your reactions to the book.

- What did you like and/or dislike about the book?

- Did you relate to the story?

- Would you recommend that a friend read this book? Why or why not?

- Would you read another book written by this same author? Why or why not?

Posting the Book Review

1. When all the reviews are written, your teacher will group the class by genre.

2. Once you are with your group, take turns copying and pasting reviews onto the main page for that genre. Only one person can edit a wiki page at a time.

3. While you are waiting, read reviews posted by other students.

4. Leave a comment for each review you read.

6 WORKING IN A BLOG

Instructional Objectives

Students will be able to:

- Set up an account for a class blog host.

- Log in to a class blog and add a comment.

Time frame: 20–25 minutes

Structure: whole class and individual

IRA/NCTE Standard

Standard 8—Students use a variety of technological and information resources (e.g., libraries, databases, computer networks, video) to gather and synthesize information and to create and communicate knowledge.

NETS*S Standard

Standard 6. Technology Operations and Concepts—Students demonstrate a sound understanding of technology concepts, systems, and operations.

Framework for 21st Century Learning

ICT Literacy—Use technology as a tool to research, organize, evaluate and communicate information.

Materials/Hardware/Software

- Student Activity Page (one copy per student)

- One Internet-connected desktop or laptop computer per student

- Classroom blog

  Blog hosts frequently used by educators include:

  - WordPress.com (http://wordpress.com)

  - Class Blogmeister (http://classblogmeister.com/)

  - EduBlogs (http://edublogs.org)

Teacher Preparation

Prior to teaching this lesson, you need to do the following:

1. To keep blog work manageable, set up a classroom blog for each class period.

2. Depending on the blog host you select, students may need individual accounts to post comments on the blog. Use of individual accounts brings accountability, as students are not able to make inappropriate anonymous comments. It will save time to have students set up their own individual accounts at the beginning of this lesson. Consult your district's Acceptable Use Policy to make sure this is permissible. If not, you will need to set up individual accounts and assign one to each student.

3. Add the URL for the blog host site and the URL for the blog to the Student Activity Page before duplicating that page. Remember, each class period's blog will have its own individual URL.

4. Create an initial post called "Welcome" in each class period blog. This will appear at the top of the blog page. Students will respond to this post as part of this activity, so be sure to end the post with a request that they write a reply.

5. Check to be sure that each student has a current, signed Acceptable Use Policy on file.

6. Arrange for students to have one-to-one access to Internet-connected desktop or laptop computers for this activity. This may require scheduling lab time or borrowing a laptop cart.

Prerequisite Student Skills

Students need to know how to:

1. Open a Web browser

2. Enter a URL in the address bar and navigate to a Web site

3. Log in to the class blog site

Vocabulary

blog: The word *blog* is a shortening of the term "Web log." A blog is a Web site that resembles an online journal. Entries appear in reverse chronological order (newest posts are at the top of the page). Typical blogs have one main author, but readers are able to write and publish comments in response to entries.

blog host: an online service that provides an application subscribers use to create their own blogs. The host also stores the blog on a server for ongoing access. Although each blog application will have a few unique features, nearly all offer the same basic capabilities for creating and editing interactive online journals.

Teaching Tips

- Blogs typically have just one author, but multiple visitors are able to read and comment on a post at the same time. This makes blogging very classroom friendly. Some blog hosts do allow blog creators to add multiple authors who can not only respond to existing posts but also create and publish original entries.

- Your "welcome message" should include an engaging question that students can respond to. For example, you might ask them to post their own ideas about ways to use the blog in class.

- Go through this activity yourself before assigning it to students. This will help you anticipate problems that might arise.

Activities/Procedures

1. **Accessing the Blog**—Distribute the Student Activity Page. Ask students to open the Web browser and use the blog host URL written on the activity sheet to navigate to the blog host site. If you are having students create their own individual blog accounts, do that now. Once students have made a note of their account information, have them navigate to the class blog. (approximately 10 minutes)

2. **Blog Overview**—Once students have accessed the class blog, ask them to take a few minutes to look at the features and read the Welcome post. Remind students that when using a school blog, they must be respectful of one another, may not use inappropriate language, and are not to post private information. (approximately 5 minutes)

3. **Responding to a Post**—Ask students to click on the Comment or Reply button, and then write and post a reply to the Welcome post. (approximately 5 minutes)

Assessment/Evaluation

- Monitor students while they are working.

- Check comments to see if students successfully wrote and posted a comment.

- Read comments to ensure that responses are appropriate and complete.

Follow-up Activities

- Poetry Anthology

- What a Character!

- Book Study

- Interactive News

Meeting the Needs of Diverse Learners

You might find that students with different abilities will benefit from extra help or extra challenges.

- Students who need extra help will benefit from working through this activity with a partner. Also, because the blog is online, these students can continue to practice these skills anywhere they have access to the Internet.

- Students who would benefit from extra challenges can explore existing guidelines for posting on classroom blogs. An example may be found at Blogging Rules on Bud the Teacher's wiki (http://budtheteacher.com/wiki/index.php?title=Blogging_Rules). These students could then create suggested class guidelines for writing replies on your class blog.

Recommended Internet Sites

- WordPress.com (http://wordpress.com)

- Class Blogmeister (http://classblogmeister.com)

- EduBlogs (http://edublogs.org)

Answer Key

There are no right or wrong answers for this activity. Check student comments to make sure they are appropriate and complete.

6 WORKING IN A BLOG

Objective

During this activity, you will log in to a class blog, review the features of the blog, and write a comment in response to an entry posted by your teacher.

Before You Begin

The word *blog* is a shortening of the term "Web log." A blog is a Web site that resembles an online journal. Entries appear in reverse chronological order. The newest posts are at the top of the page. Typical blogs have one main author. Readers are able to write and publish comments in response to entries.

Did you realize that you can use a blog for schoolwork? The purpose of this activity is to ensure that you have the basic technology skills required to use a classroom blog for collaborative and individual work.

Materials

- Student Activity Page
- Blog host URL: _____
- Class blog URL: _____
- Log-in information: _____

Directions

Accessing the Blog

1. Open the computer's Web browser. Use the blog host URL provided to get to the blog host site.

2. Follow the directions your teacher provides to set up a blog access account. You will use this to log in and to post a comment on the class blog.

3. Once you have an account, give your account user name to your teacher.

4. Use the class blog URL provided to get to the class blog.

Blog Overview

1. Take a minute to look at your class blog to see the features currently available. Follow along as your teacher provides a quick overview of the blog.

2. Read the Welcome entry posted by your teacher.

3. Look for any navigation aids. These may be links to older posts that are categorized by topic or date that make it easy to find older entries.

4. Look for a tab or link labeled **About**. If there is one, click on it. Read what you find. You should find information about the blog or the blog's author.

5. Look for a list of links to other blogs, wikis, or other online resources. These links are usually placed in a column on the left or right side of the main blog entries.

Responding to a Post

Your class blog is set up to allow students to make comments on posts written by your teacher. To complete this activity, you need to:

1. Read the Welcome post.

2. Click on **Comment** or **Reply**.

3. Click in the text box that appears.

4. Type your comment. Be sure to use complete sentences.

5. Check spelling and grammar.

6. Click on **Post** or **Submit**.

Remember, all comments posted on this blog are identified by user name. Post responsibly.

7 POETRY ANTHOLOGY

Instructional Objectives

Students will be able to:

- Write a poem in the form specified in a blog entry posted by the teacher.

- Post the poem as a comment on the teacher's original entry in the class blog.

- Read several poems posted by classmates and post a comment on one.

Time frame: 40–45 minutes

Structure: individual

IRA/NCTE Standards

Standard 6—Students apply knowledge of language structure, language conventions (e.g., spelling and punctuation), media techniques, figurative language, and genre to create, critique, and discuss print and non-print texts.

Standard 8—Students use a variety of technological and information resources (e.g., libraries, databases, computer networks, video) to gather and synthesize information and to create and communicate knowledge.

NETS*S Standards

Standard 1. Creativity and Innovation—Students demonstrate creative thinking, construct knowledge, and develop innovative products and processes using technology.

Standard 6. Technology Operations and Concepts—Students demonstrate a sound understanding of technology concepts, systems, and operations.

Framework for 21st Century Learning

Core Subjects and 21st Century Themes—Mastery of core subjects and 21st century themes is essential for students in the 21st century.

ICT Literacy—Use technology as a tool to research, organize, evaluate and communicate information.

Materials/Hardware/Software

- Student Activity Page (one copy per student)

- Teacher-created blog entry describing assignment and prompt (To set up a blog, refer to the Teacher Preparation section of Lesson 6, Working in a Blog.)

- Language Arts textbooks or other print and online reference materials with which students can find descriptions of poetry forms and examples

- Writing paper

- One Internet-connected desktop or laptop computer per student

Teacher Preparation

Remember, if you are working with multiple blogs, you will need to repeat the preparation steps for each blog.

Prior to teaching this lesson, you need to do the following:

1. Decide which poetry form students will use in this initial poetry-writing assignment (e.g., haiku, cinquain, diamante, tanka).

2. Review the textbooks and other print and online reference materials for descriptions of poetry forms and examples.

3. Write and post a blog entry that identifies the chosen poetry form. Provide simple directions for posting individual poems and commenting on classmates' work. Add any links to online reference materials students might use. If possible, add a category and/or tag to this post (e.g., Poetry) so it is easier to retrieve later.

4. Add the URL for the class blog and the title of your original entry to the Student Activity Page before duplicating that page.

5. Arrange for each student to have access to an Internet-connected desktop or laptop computer for this activity. This may require scheduling lab time or borrowing a laptop cart.

   Note: This assignment could also be completed using an Internet-connected handheld device such as a cell phone.

Prerequisite Student Skills

Students need to be familiar with:

1. How to log in to the class blog and add comments

2. The organizing principles of the chosen poetry form assigned for this activity

Vocabulary

blog: The word *blog* is a shortening of the term "Web log." A blog is a Web site that resembles an online journal. Entries appear in reverse chronological order (newest posts are at the top of the page). Typical blogs have one main author, but readers are able to write and publish comments in response to entries.

poetry form: A poetry form consists of the organizing principles that make one type of poem different from another. For example, haiku poems are three unrhymed lines of five, seven, and five syllables. Tanka poems consist of five lines; the first and third lines have five syllables each and the other three lines have seven syllables each.

Teaching Tips

- Because blogs allow many readers to simultaneously post comments to an entry, students will be able to work individually and all add their work to the blog in a short period of time. And, once the initial work is done, students may access the blog from any Internet-connected computer to add more comments.

- Many bloggers prefer to do their original writing off-line or in a word processing program. This facilitates editing the writing and protects authors from losing their work if the Internet connection is interrupted before the comment is posted. The Student Activity Sheet suggests that students who wish to initially compose their poems off-line use a sheet of paper or a word processing program. However, it is also perfectly acceptable for students to do their preliminary writing in the blog text box. If they choose the latter, remind students to check their work carefully before clicking the Submit button.

Activities/Procedures

1. **Accessing the Blog**—Distribute the Student Activity Page. Ask students to open the Web browser and use the URL written on the activity sheet to navigate to the blog. Unless you have written and posted another entry since preparing for this lesson, your entry describing the assignment should be at the top of the entry column. (approximately 5 minutes)

2. **Composing and Posting a Poem**—Your entry for this lesson should include a definition of the poetry form students are to use for the assignment. If you have provided reference materials or want students to use an online reference, that information should be included here. Review the assignment with students and then provide time for them to write and post their poems. (approximately 25 minutes)

3. **Adding a Comment**—Give students a few minutes to review and comment on one poem posted by a classmate. (approximately 10 minutes)

Assessment/Evaluation

- Monitor students while they are working.

- Read student poems to check for form and content.

- Check comments posted about poems. Are they constructive? Are they helpful?

Follow-up Activities

- This assignment can be repeated several times using various poetry forms. It is especially helpful to use categories or tags to easily track all poetry-related activities. Eventually, these poems can be downloaded and saved to create an anthology.

- Encourage students to use comments to interact with one another and engage in deeper conversations about their poetry.

Meeting the Needs of Diverse Learners

You might find that students with different abilities will benefit from extra help or extra challenges.

- Students who need extra help will benefit from completing this assignment on paper or in a word processing program before working online.

- Students who would benefit from extra challenges can review and comment on poems written by several classmates. Remind these students that this is an opportunity for them to model norms for discussing other students' work.

Recommended Internet Sites

- Types of Poetry (www.types-of-poetry.org.uk)
- Poetry for Kids (www.kathimitchell.com/poemtypes.html)

Answer Key

Answers will vary. Accept all reasonable responses.

7 POETRY ANTHOLOGY

Objective

During this activity, you will write a poem using a specific form described in a class blog post. Then you will publish your poem as a reply to the post. You will also read and comment on a poem posted by a classmate.

Before You Begin

Poetry forms are the organizing "rules" that make one type of poem different from another. For example, **haiku** poems are three unrhymed lines of five, seven, and five syllables. **Tanka** poems have five lines. The first and third lines have five syllables each. The other three lines have seven syllables each.

Using a blog, it is possible to publish poetry online that you have written for an assignment. Classmates, parents, and others can then read and comment on the work. Once an assignment is finished, bloggers can still access the post to use as a reference or model for other assignments.

Materials

- Student Activity Page
- Blog URL: _____
- Entry title (provided by your teacher): _____
- Descriptions of poetry forms and examples from Language Arts textbooks and other reference material
- Writing paper

Directions

Accessing the Blog

1. Open the computer's Web browser.

2. Use the blog URL provided to get to the classroom blog.

3. Read your teacher's post. It will describe this activity and the poetry form you are to use. Notice that you will post your poem as a reply or comment to *this* entry from your teacher.

Composing and Posting a Poem

1. Follow along as your teacher gives a brief overview of this activity.

2. Write a draft of your poem. Use another sheet of paper or create a word processing document for your draft.

3. Proofread your work.

4. Log in to the blog.

5. Post your poem as a comment. Again, be sure you proofread carefully. Click on **Post** or **Submit**.

Adding a Comment

1. Read several of the poems posted by your classmates.

2. Choose a poem to make a comment about. Click on **Comment** or **Reply** for that poem.

3. Write your comment. Keep in mind that the comment needs to be constructive and helpful.

4. Proofread your comment. Click on **Post** or **Submit** to post the comment.

Remember, comments are not anonymous.

WHAT A CHARACTER!

Instructional Objectives

Students will be able to:

- Write a brief description of a character in a literary work.

- Write a diary entry about an event in the literary work from the perspective of that character.

- Post the description and diary entry as a comment to an original blog entry written by the teacher.

- Read blog entries posted by classmates and post a comment on one.

Time frame: 40–45 minutes

Structure: individual

IRA/NCTE Standards

Standard 3—Students apply a wide range of strategies to comprehend, interpret, evaluate, and appreciate texts. They draw on their prior experience, their interactions with other readers and writers, their knowledge of word meaning and of other texts, their word identification strategies, and their understanding of textual features (e.g., sound-letter correspondence, sentence structure, context, graphics).

Standard 8—Students use a variety of technological and information resources (e.g., libraries, databases, computer networks, video) to gather and synthesize information and to create and communicate knowledge.

NETS*S Standards

Standard 1. Creativity and Innovation—Students demonstrate creative thinking, construct knowledge, and develop innovative products and processes using technology.

Standard 2. Communication and Collaboration—Students use digital media and environments to communicate and work collaboratively, including at a distance, to support individual learning and contribute to the learning of others.

Framework for 21st Century Learning

Communication and Collaboration—Articulate thoughts and ideas effectively using oral, written and nonverbal communication skills in a variety of forms and contexts.

Creativity and Innovation—Be open and responsive to new and diverse perspectives; incorporate group input and feedback into the work.

Materials/Hardware/Software

- Student Activity Page (one copy per student)

- Teacher-created blog entry describing the assignment and giving the prompt (If you need to set up a blog, refer to the Teacher Preparation section of Lesson 6, Working in a Blog.)

- One copy per student of the literary work being read

- Writing paper (for drafting a short character description)

- One Internet-connected desktop or laptop computer per student

Teacher Preparation

Remember, if you are working with multiple blogs, you will need to repeat the preparation steps for each blog.

Prior to teaching this lesson, you need to do the following:

1. Choose characters from a literary work whose identity students will assume when writing mock-diary entries.

2. Assign a character to each student. More than one student can represent the same character.

3. Write and post a blog entry that describes the overall activity. Post the first event/prompt that students will write about in character.

4. If possible, add a category and/or tag to this post (e.g., Character Responses or the title of the literary work). This will make it easier to retrieve this post later.

5. Add the URL for the class blog and the title of your original entry to the Student Activity Page before duplicating that page.

6. Arrange for each student to have access to an Internet-connected desktop or laptop computer for this activity. This may require scheduling lab time or borrowing a laptop cart.

    Note: This assignment could also be completed using an Internet-connected handheld device such as a cell phone.

Prerequisite Student Skills

Students need to be familiar with:

1. How to log in to the class blog and add comments

2. The profile of an assigned literary character

Vocabulary

blog: The word *blog* is a shortening of the term "Web log." A blog is a Web site that resembles an online journal. Entries appear in reverse chronological order (newest posts are at the top of the page). Typical blogs have one main author, but readers are able to write and publish comments in response to entries.

point of view: Every story is told from an identifiable perspective, usually through the eyes of a character. This perspective is called point of view.

Teaching Tips

- Because blogs allow many readers to simultaneously post comments to an entry, students will be able to work individually and all add their work to the blog in a short period of time. And, once the initial work is done, students may access the blog from any Internet-connected computer to add more comments.

- This activity should be the first in a series of posts that identify events for students to write about in character throughout the reading of the literary work.

Activities/Procedures

1. **Writing a Character Description**—Before accessing the blog, assign students to write a brief description of their assigned character. Students will add this description to the beginning of their first response written in character. (approximately 10 minutes)

2. **Accessing the Blog**—Distribute the Student Activity Page. Ask students to open the Web browser and use the URL written on the activity sheet to navigate to the blog. Unless you have written and posted another entry since preparing for this lesson, your entry describing the assignment should be at the top of the entry column. (approximately 5 minutes)

3. **Composing and Posting a Response**—For the teacher entry, include a brief explanation of the reason for blogging from the perspectives of various characters. Provide guidelines for what students need to include in this first comment. For example, students should include a short character description and a diary entry about the first event. Review the activity with students and then provide time for them to write and post their responses. (approximately 15 minutes)

4. **Adding a Comment**—Give students time to review and comment on a classmate's post. (approximately 10 minutes)

Assessment/Evaluation

- Monitor students while they are working.

- Read students' character descriptions to check for accuracy.

- Check diary entries. Are students staying in character when they write? Are different characters actually stating different points of view?

Follow-up Activities

This activity should be the first of several as students compose diary entries about events throughout the reading of the literary work. It is especially helpful to use categories or tags to easily track all related entries. Encourage students to use comments to interact with one another and engage in deeper conversations about their characters and their differing points of view.

Meeting the Needs of Diverse Learners

You might find that students with different abilities will benefit from extra help or extra challenges.

- Students who need extra help will benefit from creating a character development chart to fully develop their ideas about the character prior to writing their blog entries.

- Students who would benefit from extra challenges can compare and contrast their responses with others that represent the same character. How are they alike and how are they different? Did some identify a point they missed?

Recommended Internet Site

- Exploring Point of View (www.learner.org/interactives/literature/read/pov1.html)

Answer Key

Answers will vary. Accept all reasonable responses.

8

WHAT A CHARACTER!

Objectives

During this activity you will:

- Write a brief description of the character assigned by your teacher.

- Write a diary entry about an event in the literary work from the perspective of this character.

- Post your brief description and diary entry as a comment to the original blog entry written by your teacher.

- Read the blog descriptions and responses posted by classmates and post a comment on one.

Before You Begin

Every story is told from a certain point of view. One point of view is through the eyes of a character. Consider that a story can be changed a lot simply by telling it from another character's viewpoint. Imagine telling the story of Goldilocks and the Three Bears from the point of view of the baby bear, the father bear, or the mother bear. How would the description of what happened change?

Materials

- Student Activity Page

- Blog URL: _____

- Entry title: _____

- Character assigned: _____

- Writing paper

- Your copy of the literary work being read

Directions

Writing a Character Description

On a sheet of writing paper, write a brief description of the character you are assigned. You will add the description to the blog before adding the diary entry.

Accessing the Blog

1. Open the Web browser. Use the URL provided by your teacher to get to the class blog.

2. Read the entry posted by your teacher. The post describes this activity, including the event you are to respond to in character.

3. Ask any questions you may have about posting your character description and diary entry as a reply to or comment on your teacher's post.

Composing and Posting a Response

1. Think about the event you will respond to in character.

2. Outline your answer on the same sheet of paper you used to write your character description.

3. When ready to post your entry, click on **Comment** or **Reply**.

4. Type your brief character description and then your diary entry. Don't forget, your entry is written from the perspective of your character, not your own personal opinion.

5. Proofread your comment.

6. Click on **Post** or **Submit** to post your entry.

Adding a Comment

1. Read several of the entries posted by your classmates.

2. Choose one to comment on.

3. Click on **Comment** or **Reply** for that entry.

4. Write your comment. Keep in mind that the comment needs to be constructive and helpful. Proofread and edit your comment.

5. When the comment is finished, click on **Post** or **Submit**.

BOOK STUDY

Instructional Objectives

Students will be able to:

- Write a response to a prompt about a work of nonfiction being read for class.

- Post the response as a comment to an original blog entry written by the teacher.

- Read blog responses posted by classmates and post a comment about one.

Time frame: 25–30 minutes

Structure: individual

IRA/NCTE Standards

Standard 3—Students apply a wide range of strategies to comprehend, interpret, evaluate, and appreciate texts. They draw on their prior experience, their interactions with other readers and writers, their knowledge of word meaning and of other texts, their word identification strategies, and their understanding of textual features (e.g., sound-letter correspondence, sentence structure, context, graphics).

Standard 8—Students use a variety of technological and information resources (e.g., libraries, databases, computer networks, video) to gather and synthesize information and to create and communicate knowledge.

NETS*S Standards

Standard 1. Creativity and Innovation—Students demonstrate creative thinking, construct knowledge, and develop innovative products and processes using technology.

Standard 2. Communication and Collaboration—Students use digital media and environments to communicate and work collaboratively, including at a distance, to support individual learning and contribute to the learning of others.

Framework for 21st Century Learning

Communication and Collaboration—Articulate thoughts and ideas effectively using oral, written and nonverbal communication skills in a variety of forms and contexts.

Creativity and Innovation—Be open and responsive to new and diverse perspectives; incorporate group input and feedback into the work.

Materials/Hardware/Software

- Student Activity Page (one copy per student)

- Teacher-created blog entry describing the assignment and posing the prompt for students (If you need to set up a blog, refer to the Teacher Preparation section of Lesson 6, Working in a Blog.)

- One copy per student of an assigned nonfiction work

- One Internet-connected desktop or laptop computer per student

Teacher Preparation

Remember, if you are working with multiple blogs, you will need to repeat the preparation steps for each blog.

Prior to teaching this lesson, you need to do the following:

1. Develop the prompt for this first book study activity.

2. Write and post a blog entry that describes the activity and includes the prompt to which students need to respond.

3. If possible, add a category and/or tag to this post (e.g., Book Study or the title of the nonfiction work) so it is easier to retrieve later.

4. Add the URL for the class blog and the title of your original entry to the Student Activity Page before duplicating that page.

5. Arrange for each student to have access to an Internet-connected desktop or laptop computer for this activity. This may require scheduling lab time or borrowing a laptop cart.

   Note: This assignment could also be completed using an Internet-connected handheld device such as a cell phone.

Prerequisite Student Skills

Students need to be familiar with:

1. How to log in to the class blog and add comments

2. The chapter or section of the book that the prompt addresses

Vocabulary

blog: The word *blog* is a shortening of the term "Web log." A blog is a Web site that resembles an online journal. Entries appear in reverse chronological order (newest posts are at the top of the page). Typical blogs have one main author, but readers are able to write and publish comments in response to entries.

Teaching Tips

- This activity should be the first in a series of posts that ask students to respond to prompts about a nonfiction work they are reading in class.

- Because blogs allow many readers to simultaneously post comments to an entry, students will be able to work individually and all add their work to the blog in a short period of time. And, once the initial work is done, students may access the blog from any Internet-connected computer to add more comments.

Activities/Procedures

1. **Accessing the Blog**—Distribute the Student Activity Page. Ask students to open the Web browser and use the URL written on the activity sheet to navigate to the blog. Unless you have written and posted another entry since preparing for this lesson, your entry describing the assignment should be at the top of the entry column. (approximately 5 minutes)

2. **Composing and Posting a Response**—The teacher entry for this activity should include directions for what students need to include in this first response and the prompt they are to respond to. Review the activity with students and then provide time for them to write and post their responses. (approximately 10 minutes)

3. **Adding a Comment**—Give students time to review and comment on one comment posted by a classmate. (approximately 10 minutes)

Assessment/Evaluation

- Monitor students while they are working.

- Read students' responses to the prompt to check for accuracy.

- Check comments posted about other students' work. Are these remarks helpful and on target?

Follow-up Activities

This activity should be the first of several as students respond to writing prompts throughout the reading of the work of nonfiction. It is especially helpful to use categories or tags to easily track all related entries. Encourage students to use comments to interact with one another and engage in deeper conversations about their reading.

Meeting the Needs of Diverse Learners

You might find that students with different abilities will benefit from extra help or extra challenges.

- Students who need extra help will benefit from discussing the prompt with one or two other students before completing their responses.

- Students who would benefit from extra challenges can help prepare future prompts.

Recommended Internet Sites

You may find it helpful to visit sites that explain how to set up online book studies. These sites are for teacher use, not students.

- Book-Clubs-Resource.com (www.book-clubs-resource.com)

- Online Book Club (http://onlinebookclub.org)

- Shelfari (www.shelfari.com)

Answer Key

Answers will vary. Accept all reasonable responses.

9 BOOK STUDY

Objectives

During this activity you will:

- Write a response to a prompt about a work of nonfiction you are reading for class.

- Post the response as a comment to an original blog entry written by your teacher.

- Read blog responses posted by your classmates and post a comment about one.

Before You Begin

Read the chapter or section of the book. Blogs make it easy to turn this individual activity into an online group book study. You can respond to online prompts about the reading. You can also read and react to ideas posted by other students.

Materials

- Student Activity Page

- Blog URL: _____

- Entry title (provided by your teacher): _____

- Your copy of the work of nonfiction

Directions

Accessing the Blog

1. Open the Web browser. Use the URL provided by your teacher to get to the class blog.

2. Read the blog entry posted by your teacher. The post describes this assignment.

3. Ask any questions you may have about the assignment.

Composing and Posting a Response

1. Read the prompt you are to respond to in writing.

2. Think about your answer. Outline your answer below or on a separate sheet of paper.

3. When ready, click on **Comment** or **Reply**.

4. Type your response online in the blog comment text box.

5. Proofread and edit your comment.

6. Click on **Post** or **Submit**.

Adding a Comment

1. Read several of the entries posted by your classmates.

2. Choose one on which to comment.

3. Click on **Comment** or **Reply**.

4. Write your comment. Keep in mind that the comment needs to be constructive and helpful.

5. Proofread and edit your comment.

6. When the comment is finished, click on **Post** or **Submit**.

10 INTERACTIVE NEWS

Instructional Objectives

Students will:

- Read a brief online news story taken from a commercial or professional news blog plus several sample comments posted about the article.

- Working with a partner, use an informal rubric to determine the value of the sample comments.

- Individually, write and post in the class blog a conclusion about how much weight readers should give to these comments.

- Read and respond to at least one blog comment posted by a classmate.

Time frame: 40–45 minutes

Structure: partners and individual

IRA/NCTE Standards

Standard 3—Students apply a wide range of strategies to comprehend, interpret, evaluate, and appreciate texts. They draw on their prior experience, their interactions with other readers and writers, their knowledge of word meaning and of other texts, their word identification strategies, and their understanding of textual features (e.g., sound-letter correspondence, sentence structure, context, graphics).

Standard 8—Students use a variety of technological and information resources (e.g., libraries, databases, computer networks, video) to gather and synthesize information and to create and communicate knowledge.

NETS*S Standards

Standard 1. Creativity and Innovation—Students demonstrate creative thinking, construct knowledge, and develop innovative products and processes using technology.

Standard 2. Communication and Collaboration—Students use digital media and environments to communicate and work collaboratively, including at a distance, to support individual learning and contribute to the learning of others.

Framework for 21st Century Learning

Communication and Collaboration—Articulate thoughts and ideas effectively using oral, written and nonverbal communication skills in a variety of forms and contexts.

Creativity and Innovation—Be open and responsive to new and diverse perspectives; incorporate group input and feedback into the work.

Information Literacy—Evaluate information critically and competently.

Materials/Hardware/Software

- Student Activity Page (one copy per student)

- Print copies (one per student) of an online news article from a blog along with a sampling of four or five comments posted about the article. Choose comments that vary in quality and readability.

- Teacher-created blog entry summarizing the news article reviewed. (If you need to set up a blog, refer to the Teacher Preparation section of Lesson 6, Working in a Blog.)

- One Internet-connected desktop or laptop computer per student

Teacher Preparation

Remember, if you are working with multiple blogs, you will need to repeat the preparation steps for each blog.

Prior to teaching this lesson, you need to do the following:

1. Select a news article posted in a commercial or professional news blog along with four or five comments posted by readers. If possible, choose a range of comments from well-conceived, articulate samples to those with misspellings and incomplete or poorly phrased ideas.

2. Print the article and sample comments (one copy per student).

   Note: Many blogs of this type require registration to post comments. Subscribing to the blog may be both time-consuming and a violation of your school or district Acceptable Use Policy (AUP). Instead, write and post a blog entry that summarizes the article. Students will post their conclusions about the comments here.

3. If possible, add a category and/or tag to this post (e.g., Current Events or the title of the article) so it is easier to retrieve later.

4. Add the URL for the class blog and the title of your original entry to the Student Activity Page before duplicating that page.

5. Arrange for each student to have access to an Internet-connected desktop or laptop computer for this activity. This may require scheduling lab time or borrowing a laptop cart.

Prerequisite Student Skills

Students need to be familiar with:

1. How to log in to the class blog and add comments

2. The notion that comments posted online may not be valid

Vocabulary

blog: The word *blog* is a shortening of the term "Web log." A blog is a Web site that resembles an online journal. Entries appear in reverse chronological order (newest posts are at the top of the page). Typical blogs have one main author, but readers are able to write and publish comments in response to entries.

Teaching Tip

This activity can be done more than once.

Activities/Procedures

1. **Laying the Groundwork**—Distribute the Student Activity Page and the copy of the article and sample comments. Provide an overview of the steps students will take to complete this activity. Students begin by reading the article and comments. Using the simple rubric on the activity page, students work with a partner to decide if each comment meets all the criteria (yes or no for each comment). (approximately 15 minutes)

2. **Accessing the Blog**—Students open the Web browser and use the URL written on the activity sheet to navigate to the blog. Unless you have written and posted another entry since preparing for this lesson, your entry describing the assignment should be at the top of the entry column. (approximately 5 minutes)

3. **Composing and Posting a Conclusion About the Reader Comments**—Working individually, students compose and post a conclusion about the weight readers should give to the posted comments. (approximately 15 minutes)

4. **Adding a Comment**—Give students time to review and comment on at least one comment posted by a classmate. (approximately 5 minutes)

Assessment/Evaluation

- Monitor students while they are working.

- Check students' ratings of the sample comments.

- Check comments posted by the students to see if they draw reasonable conclusions about the reader posts.

Follow-up Activities

If it is not a violation of your school or district AUP, you may decide you want students to subscribe to a reputable commercial or professional blog which they can read and contribute comments to on an ongoing basis.

Meeting the Needs of Diverse Learners

You might find that students with different abilities will benefit from extra help or extra challenges.

- Students who need extra help will benefit from reading news blogs written explicitly for young readers such as http://kidsblogs.nationalgeographic.com/kidsnews.

- Students who would benefit from extra challenges can peer-review four or five comments posted by classmates.

Recommended Internet Sites

You may find it helpful to visit news sites that allow readers to comment on articles. Here are three examples:

- Chicago Tribune (www.chicagotribune.com)

- CNN (www.cnn.com)—Articles often include links to blog comments about a topic.

- TIME magazine blogs (www.time.com/time/blogs)

You may wish to pre-select an article from a news site in order to screen the comments for appropriate content before sharing with students. Controversial topics may inspire comments that are unsuitable for classroom review.

Answer Key

Answers will vary depending upon the article and comments reviewed. Accept all reasonable responses.

10 INTERACTIVE NEWS

Objectives

During this activity you will:

- Read a brief news story taken from a news Web site or news blog as well as several sample comments readers have posted about the article.

- Work with a partner to use a simple rubric to determine the value of the sample comments.

- Write and post your own conclusion on your class blog about how much weight should be given to the readers' comments you reviewed.

- Read and respond to at least one blog comment posted by a classmate.

Before You Begin

Blogs have made an impact on news reports. Average people have become "citizen reporters." One worry about news blogs is that some posts often have little or no factual information. In addition, opinions often seem like news.

Often, readers freely trust comments as if they were carefully researched articles. Expert writers are concerned about this. As a consumer of online news, the reader has a responsibility to evaluate how trustworthy a posted comment is.

Materials

- Student Activity Page

- Blog URL: _____

- Entry title (provided by your teacher): _____

- Your copy of the article and sample comments

Directions

Laying the Groundwork

1. Read the article and sample comments.

2. Work with a partner. Use the simple rubric that follows to decide which of the criteria each comment meets.

Simple Comment Rubric					
Read the criteria listed in the left column. If the comment meets that criteria, write a "Y" in the column for that comment. If the comment does not meet that criteria, write an "N" in the column for that comment.					
Criteria	Comment 1	Comment 2	Comment 3	Comment 4	Comment 5
The author of the comment identifies himself/ herself using what appears to be a real name.					
The author includes background information or credentials that show how she/he is qualified to comment on this topic.					
The author includes citations or links to easily checked resources to support his/her statement.					
The author presents ideas clearly and concisely, using appropriate language.					
The author uses accepted conventions for spelling and grammar.					

Accessing the Blog

1. Open the Web browser.

2. Use the URL provided to get to the blog.

3. Find the title for the entry describing this assignment.

4. Read the assignment and the prompt.

Composing and Posting a Conclusion About the Reader Comments

1. Read the prompt for which you are to write a response.

2. Working on your own, compose and post a conclusion about the weight you think readers should give to the sample posted comments, based upon your rubric review.

3. Outline your answer on the back of this activity sheet or on another sheet of paper.

4. When ready, click on **Comment** or **Reply**.

5. Type your response online in the blog comment text box.

6. Proofread and edit your comment.

7. Click on **Post** or **Submit**.

Adding a Comment

1. Read several of the entries posted by your classmates.

2. Choose one on which to comment.

3. Click on **Comment** or **Reply**.

4. Write your comment. Keep in mind that the comment needs to be constructive and helpful.

5. Proofread and edit your comment.

6. Click on **Post** or **Submit**.

11 USING A WEB-BASED WORD PROCESSOR

Instructional Objectives

Students will be able to:

- Log in to a Web-based application site.

- Create a new Web-based word processing document.

- Use basic editing features of the Web-based word processor.

- Invite the teacher and a classmate to be collaborators on a document.

- Add text to a document where the student is an invited collaborator.

Time frame: 45–50 minutes

Structure: whole class, individual, and partners

IRA/NCTE Standard

Standard 8—Students use a variety of technological and information resources (e.g., libraries, databases, computer networks, video) to gather and synthesize information and to create and communicate knowledge.

NETS*S Standard

Standard 6. Technology Operations and Concepts—Students demonstrate a sound understanding of technology concepts, systems, and operations.

Framework for 21st Century Learning

ICT Literacy—Use technology as a tool to research, organize, evaluate and communicate information.

Materials/Hardware/Software

- Student Activity Page (one copy per student)

- One Internet-connected desktop or laptop computer per student

- Web-based application site
  Web-based word processors used by educators include Google Docs (http://docs.google.com), Zoho (http://zoho.com), and Buzzword (https://buzzword.acrobat.com).

Teacher Preparation

Prior to teaching this lesson, you need to do the following:

1. Review the word processing tool in two or three Web-based application suites. Be sure to read the Terms of Service (TOS), particularly anything related to age restrictions on user accounts—some sites have special requirements for use with students younger than age 13.

2. Choose one Web-based application for classroom use.

3. Students will need individual accounts to access the Web-based word processing tool. It will save time to have students set up their own accounts at the beginning of this lesson. Consult your district's Acceptable Use Policy to make sure this is permissible. If not, or if the site's TOS requires that students younger than 13 use an account established by a teacher, you will need to set up individual accounts and assign one to each student.

4. Add the URL for the Web-based application site to the Student Activity Page before duplicating that page.

5. Add your own user name to the Student Activity Page so students can invite you into the document as a collaborator.

6. Check to be sure that each student has a current, signed Acceptable Use Policy on file.

7. Arrange for students to have one-to-one access to Internet-connected desktop or laptop computers for this activity. This may require scheduling lab time or borrowing a laptop cart.

Prerequisite Student Skills

Students need to know how to:

1. Open a Web browser

2. Enter a URL in the address bar and navigate to a Web site

3. Log in to the Web-based application site

Vocabulary

Web-based application: a collection of tools that allow users to create, edit, and store different types of files online, and then, when appropriate, publish these files on the Internet. These applications usually include word processing, spreadsheet, and presentation capabilities.

Web-based word processor: Like more traditional word processors, these Web-based applications can be used to create, edit, and store documents. Unlike off-line word processors, files can be accessed from any Internet-connected computer because they are stored online. In addition, the creator of a file can share the document with other users, granting viewing or full collaboration rights. Although each Web-based word processor will have some unique features, nearly all offer the same basic capabilities for creating and editing documents.

Teaching Tips

- Web-based word processing documents are created by one author who usually invites others to view and/or edit the document. A useful feature of these documents is the history, a log of visits and changes to the document showing who accessed the file and when. This feature also allows collaborators to revert to earlier versions of the document when necessary. Teachers can use the document's history to hold students accountable for their activity in the document.

- Go through this activity yourself before assigning it to students. This will help you anticipate problems that might arise.

Activities/Procedures

1. **Accessing the Web-Based Application Site**—Distribute the Student Activity Page. Ask students to open the Web browser and use the URL written on the activity sheet to navigate to the Web-based application site. If students are creating their own individual accounts, that task should be completed now. Once students have made a note of their account information, have them navigate to the main page for the Web-based application. (approximately 10 minutes)

2. **Word Processor Overview**—Once students have accessed the main page, ask them to take a few minutes to look at the way the site is organized. Remind students that when working as writing collaborators, they must be respectful of one another's work, may not use inappropriate language, and are to make constructive suggestions or edits. (approximately 5 minutes)

3. **Creating and Working with a Document**—Each student creates a new document, enters the text provided on the Student Activity Page, and experiments with formatting tools. (approximately 15 minutes)

4. **Sharing Documents and Editing Collaboratively**—Using the teacher assurance provided on the Student Activity Sheet, each student invites the teacher to be a collaborator on his or her document. Each student also partners with a nearby student so they can invite one another to be collaborators in their documents. Then students read one another's documents and respond to the questions posed to collaborators. (approximately 15 minutes)

Assessment/Evaluation

- Monitor students while they are working.

- Check your own Web-based application account to see if students have successfully shared their documents with you and with one other student.

- Review online documents to ensure that students completed the text entry and editing activity.

Follow-up Activities

- Collaborative Notes
- Writing a Mini-Essay
- Peer Editing a Mini-Essay
- Revising a Mini-Essay

Meeting the Needs of Diverse Learners

You might find that students with different abilities will benefit from extra help or extra challenges.

- Students who need extra help will benefit from working through this activity with a partner. Also, because the document is online, these students can continue to practice these skills anywhere they have access to the Internet.

- Students who would benefit from extra challenges can create suggested class norms for working collaboratively on writing or editing a document.

Recommended Internet Sites

- Google Docs (http://docs.google.com)
- Zoho (http://zoho.com)
- Buzzword (https://buzzword.acrobat.com)

Answer Key

There are no right or wrong answers for this activity. Check student comments to make sure they are appropriate and complete.

11 USING A WEB-BASED WORD PROCESSOR

Objectives

During this activity, you will:

- Log in to a Web-based application site.

- Create a new Web-based word processing document.

- Use basic editing features of the Web-based word processor.

- Invite your teacher and a classmate to be collaborators on your document.

- Add text to a document where you are an invited collaborator.

Before You Begin

You may be familiar with computer-based word processing programs such as Microsoft Word or OpenOffice.org Writer. There are also Web-based application suites that offer online word processing. These tools are similar to more traditional word processing programs in many ways. You are able to create new documents, enter text, insert graphics, edit the text, print, and save your work.

Online word processors are a great tool for students. For example, you don't need to install a software program on your computer. Files are saved online, so you can access them from any Internet-connected computer. You can invite other people to view or collaborate on your document. This means that you and a partner, study group, or teacher can work on the same document at the same time whenever you have online access. The purpose of this activity is to ensure that you have the basic technology skills required to use an online word processor for collaborative and individual work.

Materials

- Student Activity Page

- Web-based application URL: _____

- Log-in information: _____

- Teacher's user name: _____

Directions

Accessing the Web-Based Application Site

1. Open the Web browser.

2. Use the URL provided to get to the Web-based application site.

3. If your teacher provided log-in information, use that to log in to the Web-based application site. Or, follow the directions your teacher provides to set up an individual account. You will use this for all Web-based application assignments.

4. Make a note of your account information and navigate to the main page for the Web-based application.

Word Processor Overview

Take a few minutes to look at the way the site is organized. For example, does the main page provide a space to list the documents you create? Do you see icons that link to various tools? Can you see where you need to be to create a new word processing document?

Creating and Working with a Document

1. Create a new word processing document. The Web page should now look like a traditional word processing document, including a formatting tool bar that looks something like this:

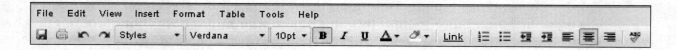

2. Add the following text to your document:

To enter text, I place the cursor over the text box, click one time, and begin to type.

When I'm done typing, I need to click on the Save button.

To add more text, I just need to place the cursor where I want to add text and then type in the additions. To format existing text, I just need to highlight the text I want to edit or change. I can click Save to keep the changes.

Student collaborator—Please answer the following questions:

1. What is your first name?

2. How could you use this online tool with a study group?

---

3. Name your document "[your first name] test".

4. **Save** the text you just typed.

5. Experiment with some of the formatting tools. For example, make a word **bold** or *italic*. Change the font or the font size. Change the text color.

6. **Save** the formatting you have added.

Sharing Documents and Editing Collaboratively

1. Invite your teacher to be a collaborator on this document. Use the teacher user name provided on this activity sheet to invite him or her.

2. Find a student partner you can invite to be a collaborator in your document.

3. Give your partner your user name so this person can invite you to be a collaborator in his or her document.

4. Invite your partner to be a collaborator.

5. View your partner's document. Answer the two collaborator questions.

6. Check spelling and grammar. Then click **Save**.

12 COLLABORATIVE NOTES

Instructional Objectives

Students will work collaboratively to:

- Create a new Web-based word processing document for an online study group.

- Invite all members and their teacher into the document as collaborators.

- Choose a note-taking format and make notes on an assigned reading.

- Notify all group members when the document is updated.

Time frame: 35–40 minutes

Structure: groups of 3–4 students

IRA/NCTE Standards

Standard 3—Students apply a wide range of strategies to comprehend, interpret, evaluate, and appreciate texts. They draw on their prior experience, their interactions with other readers and writers, their knowledge of word meaning and of other texts, their word identification strategies, and their understanding of textual features (e.g., sound-letter correspondence, sentence structure, context, graphics).

Standard 8—Students use a variety of technological and information resources (e.g., libraries, databases, computer networks, video) to gather and synthesize information and to create and communicate knowledge.

NETS*S Standards

Standard 2. Communication and Collaboration—Students use digital media and environments to communicate and work collaboratively, including at a distance, to support individual learning and contribute to the learning of others.

Standard 3. Research and Information Fluency—Students apply digital tools to gather, evaluate, and use information.

Framework for 21st Century Learning

Communication and Collaboration—Demonstrate ability to work effectively and respectfully with diverse teams.

Use and Manage Information—Manage the flow of information from a wide variety of sources.

Materials/Hardware/Software

- Student Activity Page (one copy per student)
- Short reading selection (one copy per student)
- One Internet-connected desktop or laptop computer per student

Teacher Preparation

Prior to teaching this lesson, you need to do the following:

1. Select a text for the reading assignment (one copy per student).

2. Create study groups of 3–4 students.

3. Add the URL for the Web-based application site to the Student Activity Page before duplicating that page.

4. Add your own user name to the Student Activity Page so students can invite you into the document as a collaborator.

5. Arrange for each student to have access to one Internet-connected desktop or laptop computer for this activity. This may require scheduling lab time or borrowing a laptop cart.

Prerequisite Student Skills

Students need to know how to:

1. Log in to the Web-based application site

2. Create a new word processing document and edit text

3. Add collaborators to a document

4. Notify collaborators when a document is updated

Vocabulary

collaboration: the act of working together to complete a task

Web-based word processor: Like more traditional word processors, these Web-based applications can be used to create, edit, and store documents. Unlike off-line word processors, files can be accessed from any Internet-connected computer because they are stored online. In addition, the creator of a file can share the document with other users, granting viewing or full collaboration rights. Although each Web-based word processor will have some unique features, nearly all offer the same basic capabilities for creating and editing documents.

Teaching Tips

- This activity demonstrates the power of the collaborative features of Web-based word processing. Think carefully when forming online study groups, as you may decide to continue this assignment throughout the year.

- Go through this activity yourself before assigning it to students. This will help you anticipate problems that might arise.

Activities/Procedures

1. **Accessing the Web-Based Application Site**—Distribute the Student Activity Page. Ask students to open the Web browser and use the URL written on the activity sheet to navigate to the Web-based application site. (approximately 5 minutes)

2. **Getting Started**—Each study group chooses one member to set up a document and add collaborators (study group members and teacher). While the document is being created, remaining group members agree upon the note-taking strategy they will use for this activity. (approximately 10 minutes)

3. **Taking Notes**—Each group reads and takes notes on the assigned text, using the agreed-upon format. (approximately 15 minutes)

4. **Changing Updates**—Practice notifying study group members of document updates by using the e-mail collaborators feature of the Web-based application site. (approximately 5 minutes)

Assessment/Evaluation

- Monitor students while they are working.

- Check each team page to see if the group selected a note-taking format that is appropriate for the assigned reading.

- Check each team page to ensure that notes are accurate and that all study group members have contributed to the document.

Follow-up Activities

- This activity can be repeated whenever students need to read and take notes.

- Encourage students to insert comments or add remarks using various colors for the font to differentiate among writers. The purpose of these remarks is to interact with one another and engage in deeper conversations about various aspects of the assigned reading.

Meeting the Needs of Diverse Learners

You might find that students with different abilities will benefit from extra help or extra challenges.

- When making up the teams, think about creating groups where students' strengths will complement one another, and provide support to students who might need extra help.

- Students who would benefit from extra challenges can experiment with creating and sharing Web-based templates for taking notes (e.g., Cornell method, outlining).

Recommended Internet Sites

- Note-taking systems (http://sas.calpoly.edu/asc/ssl/notetaking.systems.html#cornell)

- Academic Skills Center (www.dartmouth.edu/~acskills/success/notes.html)

Answer Key

Answers will vary depending upon the reading assigned and the note-taking format selected. Accept all reasonable responses.

12 COLLABORATIVE NOTES

Objectives

During this activity you will work collaboratively in a study group to:

- Create a new Web-based word processing document for the group.

- Invite all members and your teacher into the document as collaborators.

- Choose a note-taking format and take notes on the assigned reading.

- Notify all group members when the document is updated.

Before You Begin

Taking useful notes is a critical study skill. Using an online word processor, it is possible to work with others to take notes and to share notes. Once the notes are written, you can access them to use as a tool for review or ongoing work.

You will complete this activity with two or three classmates (as assigned by your teacher).

Materials

- Student Activity Page (one copy per student)

- Web-based application URL: _____

- Teacher's user name: _____

- User names for classmate collaborators: _____

  _____

- Short reading selection (one copy per student)

Directions

Accessing the Web-Based Application Site

1. Use the URL written on this activity sheet to get to the Web-based application site and log in.

2. Record the user names of the members of your study group on the lines provided in the materials list above.

3. Choose one member of your study group to set up a document. This person will add study group members and your teacher as collaborators.

4. While the person you chose is creating the document, agree upon the note-taking strategy you will use for this activity. You may choose from the following:

- Cornell method—a table with two columns (notes in the right column, keywords in the left column) and a summary at the bottom of the page

- Outline—taditional outline format with main ideas or topics at the left margin and subtopics or supporting ideas indented

- Paragraph—summary of the reading with the keywords highlighted

Taking Notes

1. Read the assigned text.

2. Add notes about the material using the agreed-upon format.

Changing Updates

After adding your notes to the document, practice notifying study group members of document updates. Use the e-mail collaborators feature of the Web-based application site.

13 **WRITING A MINI-ESSAY**

Instructional Objectives

Students will be able to:

- Create a new online word processing document.

- Write a brief essay in an online word processing document.

Time frame: one class period

Structure: individual

IRA/NCTE Standards

Standard 4—Students adjust their use of spoken, written, and visual language (e.g., conventions, style, vocabulary) to communicate effectively with a variety of audiences and for different purposes.

Standard 8—Students use a variety of technological and information resources (e.g., libraries, databases, computer networks, video) to gather and synthesize information and to create and communicate knowledge.

NETS*S Standard

Standard 2. Communication and Collaboration—Students use digital media and environments to communicate and work collaboratively, including at a distance, to support individual learning and contribute to the learning of others.

Framework for 21st Century Learning

Communication and Collaboration—Articulate thoughts and ideas effectively using oral, written and nonverbal communication skills in a variety of forms and contexts.

Materials/Hardware/Software

- Student Activity Page (one copy per student)

- One Internet-connected desktop or laptop computer per student team

Teacher Preparation

Prior to teaching this lesson, you need to do the following:

1. Decide on a topic for the mini-essay. This essay will consist of two to three paragraphs and be based on a topic familiar to students to facilitate completing the essay in one class period. Add the topic to the Student Activity Page before duplicating that page.

2. Create teams of 3–4 students. These students will invite each other to be collaborators in their files for the next activity.

3. Add the URL for the Web-based application site to the Student Activity Page before duplicating that page.

4. Add your own user name to the Student Activity Page so students can invite you into the document as a collaborator.

5. Arrange for each team of students to have access to one Internet-connected desktop or laptop computer. This may require scheduling lab time or borrowing a laptop cart.

Prerequisite Student Skills

Students need to know how to:

1. Log in to the Web-based application site

2. Create a new word processing document and edit text

3. Add collaborators to a document

Vocabulary

collaboration: the act of working together to complete a task

Web-based word processor: Like more traditional word processors, these Web-based applications can be used to create, edit, and store documents. Unlike off-line word processors, files can be accessed from any Internet-connected computer because they are stored online. In addition, the creator of a file can share the document with other users, granting viewing or full collaboration rights. Although each Web-based word processor will have some unique features, nearly all offer the same basic capabilities for creating and editing documents.

Teaching Tips

- If they have completed the two activities that precede this lesson, students should be very comfortable creating a new document and entering text.

- Be sure that you choose a topic familiar to students so it is easy for them to write a two- or three-paragraph essay for this activity.

Activities/Procedures

1. **Accessing the Web-Based Application Site**—Distribute the Student Activity Page. Ask students to open the Web browser and use the URL written on the activity sheet to navigate to the Web-based application site. (approximately 5 minutes)

2. **Writing the Essay**—Each student creates a new document and writes a two- to three-paragraph essay on the topic identified by the teacher. (approximately 40 minutes)

3. **Adding Collaborators**—Each student adds the teacher and two to three students (as identified by the teacher) as collaborators to her or his document. (approximately 5 minutes)

Assessment/Evaluation

- Monitor students while they are working.

- Check documents to ensure students have written their essays.

- Check to ensure that students have added classmates as collaborators.

Follow-up Activities

This lesson is the first in a series of three that ask students write a brief essay, peer edit essays written by classmates, and revise based on comments and suggestions made by classmates.

Meeting the Needs of Diverse Learners

You might find that students with different abilities will benefit from extra help or extra challenges.

- Students who need extra help will benefit from writing a shorter passage or answering a series of questions using this technology rather than writing a mini-essay.

- Students who would benefit from extra challenges can write a more in-depth essay on the same topic. In this case, make sure that the collaborators on these students' documents have also written more complex essays.

Recommended Internet Sites

Web-based applications usually have some kind of online help section. Once you have selected the Web-based word processor you want to use, review the help section to see if students would benefit from having the link to this resource.

Answer Key

Answers will vary depending upon the topic chosen. Accept all reasonable essays.

13 WRITING A MINI-ESSAY

Objective

During this activity you will use an online word processing document to write a two- to three-paragraph essay on a topic assigned by your teacher.

Before You Begin

Web-based word processors make it possible for you to write and edit text online, and then share your work with someone else. These collaborators can read your work and provide valuable feedback.

Materials

- Student Activity Page
- Web-based application URL: _____
- Essay topic: _____
- Teacher's user name: _____
- User names for classmate collaborators: _____

Directions

Accessing the Web-Based Application Site

Use the URL written on this activity sheet to navigate to the Web-based application site. Log in.

Writing the Essay

Create a new document. Write a two- to three-paragraph essay on the topic assigned by your teacher.

Adding Collaborators

Add your teacher and two to three classmates (as identified by your teacher) as collaborators to your document. Record the user names of your collaborators on the lines provided in the materials list above.

14 PEER EDITING A MINI-ESSAY

Instructional Objectives

Students will be able to:

- Use a rubric to peer edit one or more classmates' mini-essays.

- Add comments to a classmate's online word processing document as a collaborator.

Time frame: 30–60 minutes

Structure: individual

IRA/NCTE Standards

Standard 3—Students apply a wide range of strategies to comprehend, interpret, evaluate, and appreciate texts. They draw on their prior experience, their interactions with other readers and writers, their knowledge of word meaning and of other texts, their word identification strategies, and their understanding of textual features (e.g., sound-letter correspondence, sentence structure, context, graphics).

Standard 8—Students use a variety of technological and information resources (e.g., libraries, databases, computer networks, video) to gather and synthesize information and to create and communicate knowledge.

NETS*S Standard

Standard 2. Communication and Collaboration—Students use digital media and environments to communicate and work collaboratively, including at a distance, to support individual learning and contribute to the learning of others.

Framework for 21st Century Learning

Communication and Collaboration—Demonstrate ability to work effectively and respectfully with diverse teams.

Flexibility and Adaptability—Incorporate feedback effectively and deal positively with praise, setbacks and criticism.

Materials/Hardware/Software

- Student Activity Page (one copy per student)

- Saved copy of a mini-essay

- Peer editing rubric

- One Internet-connected desktop or laptop computer per student

Teacher Preparation

Prior to teaching this lesson, you need to do the following:

1. Create or select a rubric for students to use. Make copies for students. If you do not have a rubric, consider modifying the general rubric found in the introduction of this book.

2. Add the URL for the Web-based application site to the Student Activity Page before duplicating that page.

3. Arrange for each student to have access to one Internet-connected desktop or laptop computer for this activity. This may require scheduling lab time or borrowing a laptop cart.

Prerequisite Student Skills

Students need to know how to:

1. Log in to the Web-based application site

2. Access shared documents

3. Use the peer editing rubric provided

4. Insert or add comments to an online word processing document

Vocabulary

collaboration: the act of working together to complete a task

Web-based word processor: Like more traditional word processors, these Web-based applications can be used to create, edit, and store documents. Unlike off-line word processors, files can be accessed from any Internet-connected computer because they are stored online. In addition, the creator of a file can share the document with other users, granting viewing or full collaboration rights. Although each Web-based word processor will have some unique features, nearly all offer the same basic capabilities for creating and editing documents.

Teaching Tip

Be sure that you provide students a brief review of the peer editing rubric and explain how you want them to add or insert comments before they begin editing essays.

Activities/Procedures

1. **Accessing the Web-Based Application Site**—Distribute the Student Activity Page. Ask students to open the Web browser and use the URL written on the activity sheet to navigate to the Web-based application site. (no more than 5 minutes)

2. **Peer Editing the Essay**—Provide a brief review of the peer editing rubric and how you want students to add or insert comments. Each student peer edits at least one of their partners' essays. (up to 40 minutes)

3. **Reviewing the Comments Added by Collaborators**—Each student reviews the peer editor comments added to their own essays. (up to 15 minutes)

Assessment/Evaluation

- Monitor students while they are working.

- Check comments to ensure students have peer edited the essays.

Follow-up Activities

This lesson is the second in a series of three lessons in which students write a brief essay, peer edit essays written by classmates, and revise their writing based on comments and suggestions made by classmates. Encourage students to add criteria to the peer editing rubric they used and assess work based on the new criteria.

Meeting the Needs of Diverse Learners

You might find that students with different abilities will benefit from extra help or extra challenges.

- Students who need extra help will benefit from working with a partner as they peer edit classmates' essays.

- Students who would benefit from extra challenges can edit more complex essays written by classmates (see Lesson 13, Writing a Mini-Essay).

Recommended Internet Sites

Web-based applications usually have some kind of online help section. Once you have selected the Web-based word processor you want to use, review the help section to see if students would benefit from having the link to this resource, particularly information about inserting comments, if available.

- Peer Edit with Perfection (www.readwritethink.org/lessons/lesson_view.asp?id=786) Lesson plan with linked resources

- Peer Editing (www.teachersnetwork.org/NTNY/nychelp/manage/peeredit.htm) Article and links to resources

Answer Key

Answers will vary depending upon the essays being peer edited. Accept all reasonable essays.

14 PEER EDITING A MINI-ESSAY

Objective

During this activity, you will use a rubric to peer edit one or more classmates' mini-essays.

Before You Begin

The real power of Web-based word processing is in the ability to make changes to the document you create. In this activity, your collaborators will peer edit your mini-essay while you peer edit their essays. You added your teacher and your assigned collaborators to your document in the previous activity. Record their user names on the lines below.

Materials

- Student Activity Page
- Copy of peer editing rubric
- Web-based application URL: _____
- Teacher's user name: _____
- User names for classmate collaborators: _____
  _____

Directions

Accessing the Web-Based Application Site

Use the URL written on this activity sheet to navigate to the Web-based application site. Log in.

Peer Editing the Essay

1. Follow along as your teacher provides a quick review of the peer editing rubric.

2. Make sure you understand how to insert or add comments to a document.

   If the Web-based word processor supports inserting comments, you can add your remarks using this feature.

   If the Web-based word processor does not support using comments, you can add your remarks using one of the font colors other than black. In this case, be sure to add your initials to each comment so the author can easily see who made the remark.

3. Once you have been made a collaborator, edit the essay(s). Remember to make your comments constructive, not hurtful.

Reviewing the Comments Added by Your Collaborators

Review the peer editor comments added to your own essay. Remember, these comments are meant to help you improve your writing.

15 REVISING A MINI-ESSAY

Instructional Objectives

Students will be able to:

- Save a copy of a mini-essay, including copying the collaborators.

- Revise a mini-essay based on feedback provided by one or more collaborators.

Time frame: 35–45 minutes

Structure: individual

IRA/NCTE Standards

Standard 3—Students apply a wide range of strategies to comprehend, interpret, evaluate, and appreciate texts. They draw on their prior experience, their interactions with other readers and writers, their knowledge of word meaning and of other texts, their word identification strategies, and their understanding of textual features (e.g., sound-letter correspondence, sentence structure, context, graphics).

Standard 8—Students use a variety of technological and information resources (e.g., libraries, databases, computer networks, video) to gather and synthesize information and to create and communicate knowledge.

NETS*S Standard

Standard 2. Communication and Collaboration—Students use digital media and environments to communicate and work collaboratively, including at a distance, to support individual learning and contribute to the learning of others.

Framework for 21st Century Learning

Communication and Collaboration—Demonstrate ability to work effectively and respectfully with diverse teams.

Flexibility and Adaptability—Incorporate feedback effectively and deal positively with praise, setbacks and criticism.

Materials/Hardware/Software

- Student Activity Page (one copy per student)

- Saved copy of a mini-essay with comments

- One Internet-connected desktop or laptop computer per student

Teacher Preparation

Prior to teaching this lesson, you need to do the following:

1. Arrange for each student to have access to one Internet-connected desktop or laptop computer for this activity. This may require scheduling lab time or borrowing a laptop cart.

2. Make sure each student has a saved mini-essay with comments to revise.

Prerequisite Student Skills

Students need to know how to:

1. Log in to the Web-based application site

2. Access shared documents

3. Make a copy of an online document (including copying collaborators) for editing

4. Revise text based on feedback from collaborators

Vocabulary

collaboration: the act of working together to complete a task

Web-based word processor: Like more traditional word processors, these Web-based applications can be used to create, edit, and store documents. Unlike off-line word processors, files can be accessed from any Internet-connected computer because they are stored online. In addition, the creator of a file can share the document with other users, granting viewing or full collaboration rights. Although each Web-based word processor will have some unique features, nearly all offer the same basic capabilities for creating and editing documents.

Teaching Tip

If they have completed the four activities that precede this lesson, students will be very comfortable accessing and working with existing documents. Be sure that you provide students a brief review of how to save a copy of the document to edit.

Activities/Procedures

1. **Accessing the Web-Based Application Site**—Distribute the Student Activity Page. Ask students to open the Web browser and use the URL written on the activity sheet to navigate to the Web-based application site. (no more than 5 minutes)

2. **Revising the Essay**—Make certain that students understand they can use the Save As or Copy features under the File menu to make a copy of their original document. They will use this copy to make their revisions. This allows students to maintain a copy of the original essay with notes and have a final copy with all edits made. Each student reviews the comments and suggestions made by the collaborators and revises his or her essay to complete a final draft. (20 to 35 minutes)

3. **Final Reflection**—Ask students to take a few minutes to reflect on this three-part activity after they have finished the final draft. This reflection can be added at the end of the final draft of the mini-essay. (5 minutes)

Assessment/Evaluation

- Monitor students while they are working.

- Check final essays. Look at the original document to see what peer editing suggestions were incorporated into the final draft of the mini-essay.

Follow-up Activities

This lesson is the last in a series of three lessons, in which students write a brief essay, peer edit essays written by classmates, and revise their writing based on comments and suggestions made by classmates. Now that students have gone through this collaborative process one time, you can have them complete a variety of different types of writing assignments in this online environment both in class and at home.

Meeting the Needs of Diverse Learners

You might find that students with different abilities will benefit from extra help or extra challenges.

- Students who need extra help will benefit from having extra time by completing this activity as a homework assignment.

- Students who would benefit from extra challenges can revise the more complex essays they have written (see Lesson 13, Writing a Mini-Essay, and Lesson 14, Peer Editing a Mini-Essay).

Recommended Internet Sites

Web-based applications usually have some kind of online help section. Once you have selected the Web-based word processor you want to use, review the help section to see if students would benefit from having the link to this resource, particularly information about how to save a copy of a document, viewing document history, and comparing versions of the document.

Answer Key

Answers will vary depending upon the essays being revised. Accept all reasonable essays.

15 REVISING A MINI-ESSAY

Objective

During this activity you will save a copy of your mini-essay file and use that file to make final revisions. Be sure you also copy collaborators so they can read your final draft.

Before You Begin

You and your collaborators created and commented on mini-essays. Now you have an opportunity to review the collaborators' comments and suggestions. Think about how they will impact the final draft of your essay. Use your classmates' comments and suggestions to revise your essay.

　　You added your teacher and your assigned collaborators to your document in a previous activity. Record their user names on the lines provided below.

Materials

- Student Activity Page

- Web-based application URL: _____

- Teacher's user name: _____

- User names for classmate collaborators: _____

　_____

Directions

Accessing the Web-Based Application Site

Use the URL written on this activity sheet to navigate to the Web-based application site. Log in.

Revising the Essay

1. Follow along as your teacher reviews how to make a copy of your original document. You will use the copy for final editing.

2. Review the comments and suggestions made by your collaborators.

3. Revise your essay to complete a final draft. (20 to 35 minutes)

Final Reflection

Think about the revision process. Write a paragraph that describes your experience and how you felt at the end of your final draft. What do you like about this approach? What would you change? Explain.

16 USING A WEB-BASED PRESENTATION TOOL

Instructional Objectives

Students will be able to:

- Log in to a Web-based application site.

- Create a new Web-based presentation document.

- Use basic editing features of the Web-based presentation tool.

- Insert an image into a slide.

- Invite the teacher and a classmate to be collaborators in the presentation.

- Add text to a presentation where she or he is an invited collaborator.

Time frame: 45–50 minutes

Structure: whole class, individual, and partners

IRA/NCTE Standard

Standard 8—Students use a variety of technological and information resources (e.g., libraries, databases, computer networks, video) to gather and synthesize information and to create and communicate knowledge.

NETS*S Standard

Standard 6. Technology Operations and Concepts—Students demonstrate a sound understanding of technology concepts, systems, and operations.

Framework for 21st Century Learning

ICT Literacy—Use technology as a tool to research, organize, evaluate and communicate information.

Materials/Hardware/Software

- Student Activity Page (one copy per student)

- Web-based application site

  - Web-based presentation tools often used by educators include Google Docs (http://docs.google.com) and Zoho (http://zoho.com).

- Digital image (for students to use when practicing how to insert an image)

- One Internet-connected desktop or laptop computer per student

Teacher Preparation

Prior to teaching this lesson, you need to do the following:

1. Review at least two presentation tools. Be sure that the tool supports editing rights for collaborators as well as viewing rights. Read the Terms of Service (TOS) carefully, particularly anything related to age restrictions on user accounts—some sites have special requirements for use with students younger than age 13.

2. Choose one Web-based presentation tool for classroom use.

3. Set up students with login names and passwords. If students have completed the Web-based word processing activities and if you select the same Web-based application suite for this series of activities, students will already have a login name and password. Otherwise, students will need individual accounts to access the Web-based presentation tool. It will save time to have students set up their own accounts at the beginning of this lesson. Consult your district's Acceptable Use Policy to make sure this is permissible. If not, or if the site's TOS requires that students younger than 13 use an account established by a teacher, you will need to set up individual accounts and assign one to each student.

4. Add the URL for the Web-based presentation tool and your user name to the Student Activity Page before duplicating that page.

5. Upload a digital photo onto the hard drive of each student computer. If you have a class wiki, you can upload the photo to the file storage area there. If you do not have a digital image, go to Flickr (http://flickr.com). Search the Creative Commons area to find an appropriate image to upload. Be sure to read the directions for inserting an image into a slide, which you will find in the presentation tool Help section.

6. Check to be sure that each student has a current, signed Acceptable Use Policy on file.

7. Arrange for students to have one-to-one access to Internet-connected desktop or laptop computers for this activity. This may require scheduling lab time or borrowing a laptop cart.

Prerequisite Student Skills

Students need to know how to:

1. Open a Web browser

2. Enter a URL in the address bar and navigate to a Web site

3. Log in to the Web-based presentation tool

Vocabulary

Web-based application: a collection of tools that allow users to create, edit, and store different types of files online, and then, when appropriate, publish these files on the Internet. These applications usually include word processing, spreadsheet, and presentation capabilities.

Web-based presentation tool: Like more traditional presentation tools, these Web-based applications can be used to create, edit, and store presentation slides. Unlike off-line presentation tools, files can be accessed from any Internet-connected computer because they are stored online. In addition, a presentation's creator can share the file with other users, granting viewing or full collaboration rights. Although each Web-based presentation tool will have some unique features, nearly all offer the same basic capabilities for creating and editing slide shows.

Teaching Tips

- Web-based presentations are created by one person who usually invites others to view or edit the presentation. A useful feature of these files is the *history*, a log of visits and changes to the file showing who accessed it and when. This feature also allows collaborators to revert to earlier versions of the presentation when necessary. Teachers can use the history to hold students accountable for their contributions to the file.

- Most Web-based presentations are limited in the features they offer. The reason for using a tool of this type is to provide access to all students and to support collaboration on slide show projects.

- To help you anticipate problems that might arise, go through this activity yourself before assigning it to students.

Activities/Procedures

1. **Accessing the Web-Based Application Site**—Distribute the Student Activity Page. Tell students to open the Web browser and use the URL provided on the activity sheet to navigate to the Web-based application site. If students need to create individual accounts, that task should be completed now. Once students have made a note of their account information, have them navigate to the main page for the Web-based application. (approximately 10 minutes)

2. **Presentation Tool Overview**—From the main page, ask students to look at the way the site is organized, paying close attention to items that appear to be related to presentation files. Remind students that when working as a collaborator on a presentation, they must be respectful of one another's work, may not use inappropriate language, and are to make constructive suggestions or edits. (approximately 5 minutes)

3. **Creating and Working with a Presentation**—Each student creates a new presentation file, inserts the slides identified on the Student Activity Page, and experiments with formatting tools and inserting an image on one slide. Tell students how to locate the image file they will use. (approximately 15 minutes)

4. **Sharing Presentations and Editing Collaboratively**— Have each student invite you to be a collaborator on his or her document, using the teacher user name you provided on the Student Activity Sheet. Each student partners with a nearby student so they can invite one another to be collaborators in their presentations. Students review one another's slides and add the collaborator slide described on the activity sheet. (approximately 15 minutes)

Assessment/Evaluation

- Monitor students while they are working.

- Check your own Web-based application account to see if students have successfully shared their presentations with you and with one other student.

- Review online presentations to ensure that students completed the text entry and editing activity.

Follow-up Activities

- Planning a Web-Based Presentation—Brainstorming
- Planning a Web-Based Presentation—Outlining
- Planning a Web-Based Presentation—Images and Text
- Six-Word Stories

Meeting the Needs of Diverse Learners

You might find that students with different abilities will benefit from extra help or extra challenges.

- Students who need extra help will benefit from working through this activity with a partner. Before creating slides, some students may wish to create drafts on paper. Once the document is created online, students can continue to practice these skills anywhere they have access to the Internet.

- Students who would benefit from extra challenges can explore features of the presentation tool not covered in this lesson. They may create a "user's guide" which describes some of these additional features using a collaborative Web-based word processing document. This document can be published for use by the whole class.

Recommended Internet Sites

- Google Docs (http://docs.google.com)

- Zoho (http://zoho.com)

- Presentation Zen blog (http://presentationzen.blogs.com)
  Use this resource yourself to find tips and tricks for creating effective presentations. Share these ideas with students.

Answer Key

There are no right or wrong answers for this activity. Check student comments to make sure they are appropriate and complete.

16 USING A WEB-BASED PRESENTATION TOOL

Objectives

During this activity, you will:

- Log in to a Web-based application site.

- Create a new Web-based presentation document.

- Use basic editing features of the Web-based presentation tool.

- Insert an image on one slide.

- Invite your teacher and a classmate to be collaborators in the presentation.

- Add text to a presentation for which you are an invited collaborator.

Before You Begin

You may have used a computer-based presentation tool such as Microsoft PowerPoint or OpenOffice.org Impress. There are also Web-based applications that work in the same way. You can use the Web-based presentation tools to create slide shows, enter text, insert graphics, edit the text, print, and save your work.

Online presentation tools are great because users do not need to install a software program on a computer. Files are saved online. The files can be accessed from any Internet-connected computer. Users can invite other people to view or collaborate on slide shows. This means that you and a partner, a study group, or a teacher can work on the same presentation at the same time whenever you have online access. The purpose of this activity is to ensure that you have the basic technology skills needed to use an online presentation tool.

Materials

- Student Activity Page

- Web-based application URL: _____

- Log-in information (either assigned by your teacher or created by you when you first access the Web-based application): _____

- Teacher's user name: _____

Directions

Accessing the Web-Based Application Site

1. Open the Web browser. Use the URL written on the activity sheet to navigate to the Web-based application site.

2. Log in to the Web-based application site. You may need to follow the directions your teacher provides to set up an individual account to use for all Web-based application assignments.

3. Write down your account information. Navigate to the main page for the Web-based application.

Presentation Tool Overview

Take a few minutes to look at the way the site is organized. For example, does the main page provide a space to list the presentations you create? Do you see icons that link to various tools? Can you see where you need to be to create a new presentation file?

Creating and Working with a Presentation

Create a new presentation file. The Web page should now look like a traditional PowerPoint file. It should include a formatting toolbar that looks something like this:

USING A WEB-BASED PRESENTATION TOOL

Follow the directions below to create a simple slide show.

1. **Create a Title Slide**—Name your presentation after yourself; for example, "[Your first name]'s First Presentation." Add today's date in the text box below the title box.

2. **Create More Slides**—Insert two slides after the title slide. Slide 2 should have a title and a text box. Slide 3 should have a title, with the rest of the slide being blank.

3. **Add Text to Slide 2**—Title this slide "Top Tips for Slides." Think about what makes a good presentation on a slide. Read the tips listed below. Choose two. Add them to the slide in a bulleted list like this one:

   • Keep it simple.

   • Limit bullet points and text.

   • Limit use of animations.

   • Use easy-to-read fonts.

   • Use good-quality graphics.

   • Use color well.

4. **Format Slide 2**—Experiment with the formatting tools. Change the font type, size, or color. You may also explore changing the background. Have fun!

5. **Find an Image for Slide 3**—You can add images to slides. Most often you do this by saving a digital image online or on your hard drive, creating a slide where the image will be placed, and using the **Insert** command to add the image to the slide. Your teacher has chosen an image file for this activity. Listen as your teacher tells the class where to locate this file.

6. **Add an Image to Slide 3**—Insert the image on Slide 3. Add a caption or title for the image to the slide.

7. **Save** your presentation.

Sharing Presentations and Editing Collaboratively

1. Invite your teacher to be a collaborator on this document. Use your teacher's user name, provided in the materials list on the first page of this activity.

2. Invite a classmate or assigned partner to be a collaborator on your document. Record your partner's user name.

3. Give out your user name so you can be invited as a collaborator.

4. View your classmate's presentation.

5. Navigate to Slide 2. Add one additional tip to your classmate's Slide 2.

6. **Save** and **Close** the presentation file.

17 PLANNING A WEB-BASED PRESENTATION— BRAINSTORMING

Instructional Objectives

Students will work collaboratively to:

- Create a new Web-based word processing document for an online working group.

- Invite collaborators to the document.

- Choose between using a text list or Draw features to brainstorm ideas for a five-slide group presentation.

- Brainstorm ideas based on a topic presented by the teacher.

- Notify all collaborators when changes are made to the document.

Time frame: 35–40 minutes

Structure: groups of 3–4 students

IRA/NCTE Standards

Standard 5—Students employ a wide range of strategies as they write and use different writing process elements appropriately to communicate with different audiences for a variety of purposes.

Standard 8—Students use a variety of technological and information resources (e.g., libraries, databases, computer networks, video) to gather and synthesize information and to create and communicate knowledge.

NETS*S Standards

Standard 2. Communication and Collaboration—Students use digital media and environments to communicate and work collaboratively, including at a distance, to support individual learning and contribute to the learning of others.

Standard 3. Research and Information Fluency—Students apply digital tools to gather, evaluate, and use information.

Framework for 21st Century Learning

Communication and Collaboration—Demonstrate ability to work effectively and respectfully with diverse teams.

Use and Manage Information—Manage the flow of information from a wide variety of sources.

Materials/Hardware/Software

- Student Activity Page (one copy per student)
- Presentation topic (provided by teacher)
- One Internet-connected desktop or laptop computer per student

Teacher Preparation

Prior to teaching this lesson, you need to do the following:

1. Choose a broad topic for student presentations; for example, a topic based on a reading assignment, writing skill, or research theme.

2. Create working groups of 3–4 students.

3. Add the URL for the Web-based application site to the Student Activity Page before duplicating that page.

4. Provide the students' working group assignments prior to starting this lesson.

5. Arrange for each student to have access to one Internet-connected desktop or laptop computer for this activity. This may require scheduling lab time or borrowing a laptop cart.

Prerequisite Student Skills

Students need to know how to:

1. Log in to the Web-based application site

2. Create a new word processing document and edit text

3. Add collaborators to a document

Vocabulary

draw feature: This feature of a word processor allows you to add one or more drawings to a document. To insert a new drawing, you typically place the cursor where you want the drawing to appear in the document, click on Insert in the main toolbar, and then select Drawing.

Web-based word processor: Like more traditional word processors, these Web-based applications can be used to create, edit, and store documents. Unlike off-line word processors, files can be accessed from any Internet-connected computer because they are stored online. In addition, the creator of a file can share the document with other users, granting viewing or full collaboration rights. Although each Web-based word processor will have some unique features, nearly all offer the same basic capabilities for creating and editing documents.

Teaching Tips

- This activity is the first of three that demonstrate the power of the collaborative features of Web-based word processing. You can repeat this series of lessons multiple times using different topics.

- Some students will want to do their brainstorming using text, while others will prefer to use the Draw feature to make a mind map. It might be helpful to form working groups based, at least in part, on your knowledge of which method individual students are likely to favor.

- Go through this activity yourself before assigning it to students. This will help you anticipate problems that might arise.

Activities/Procedures

1. **Accessing the Web-Based Application Site**—Distribute the Student Activity Page. Ask students to open the Web browser and use the URL written on the activity sheet to navigate to the Web-based application site. (approximately 5 minutes)

2. **Getting Started**—Tell each working group to choose one member to set up a document and add collaborators (working group members and teacher). While this person is creating the document, direct remaining group members to agree upon the brainstorming strategy they will use for this activity. (approximately 10 minutes)

3. **Brainstorming**—Based on the topic you assign, have each group brainstorm ideas for presenting the topic in a five-slide presentation. Direct them to add their ideas to the shared document. (approximately 15 minutes)

4. **Adding Updates**—Work with students to practice notifying study group members of document updates. Demonstrate using the e-mail collaborators feature of the Web-based application site. (approximately 5 minutes)

Assessment/Evaluation

- Monitor students while they are working.

- Check each team document to see which brainstorming format was selected by that group.

- Check each team document to ensure that brainstorming ideas are on target and that all working group members have contributed to the document. (Check the document history for this information.)

Follow-up Activities

- This activity can be repeated whenever students need to begin a collaborative activity by brainstorming ideas.

- Encourage students to add their ideas using various font colors to differentiate among writers. The purpose of everyone working on the document is to encourage interaction and engagement in deeper conversations about various aspects of the assigned topic.

Meeting the Needs of Diverse Learners

You might find that students with different abilities will benefit from extra help or extra challenges.

- When making up the teams, think about creating groups where students' strengths will complement one another, and provide support to students who might need extra help. Suggest that some students create drafts on paper before working online.

- Students who would benefit from extra challenges can experiment with using a Web-based mind mapping tool that supports sharing files in real time such as Mindomo (www.mindomo.com) or Bubbl.us (http://bubbl.us/) to do their collaborative brainstorming.

Recommended Internet Sites

- Mindomo (www.mindomo.com)

- Bubbl.us (http://bubbl.us/)

Answer Key

Answers will vary depending on the topic assigned and the brainstorming format selected. Accept all reasonable responses.

PLANNING A WEB-BASED PRESENTATION— BRAINSTORMING

Objectives

During this activity, you will collaborate with a working group to:

- Create a new Web-based word processing document for the group.

- Invite collaborators to the document.

- Choose between using a text list or drawing a mind map to brainstorm ideas for a five-slide group presentation.

- Brainstorm ideas based on an assigned topic.

- Notify all group members when documents are changed.

Before You Begin

Creating a slide show is like writing a story. Pre-writing is an important step in putting together a presentation or a story. Pre-writing activities include generating ideas through brainstorming and creating an outline. Because a slide show is structured, planning what you will present is very important.

Complete this activity with two or three classmates. Together, you will brainstorm ideas for a given topic. You may use this list of ideas to create a formal presentation another day.

Materials

- Student Activity Page (one copy per student)

- Web-based application URL: _____

- Teacher's user name: _____

- User names for classmate collaborators: _____

  _____

- Presentation topic (assigned by your teacher): _____

Directions

Accessing the Web-Based Application Site

1. Use the URL written on this activity sheet to navigate to the Web-based application site and log in.

2. Choose one member of your working group to set up a document. This person is to add the group members and your teacher as collaborators.

3. While your group member is creating the document, the remaining group members discuss which brainstorming strategy to use. The group could make lists of ideas and then categorize the ideas into lists of related items. Or, the group could use the Draw feature to create a mind map.

4. As a group, choose a strategy.

Brainstorming

1. Brainstorm ideas for ways the group can present the topic in a five-slide presentation.

2. Assign each member of the working group one font color. Add each member's name at the top of the document in that color.

3. Each member is to work on the document. Members add their ideas to the shared document using their assigned color.

Adding Updates

1. After class, and before your group works on the next activity, continue to add ideas to the brainstorming document.

2. Every time you add something to the document, notify your group members that you made a change. Use the e-mail collaborators feature of the Web-based application site to alert them.

18 PLANNING A WEB-BASED PRESENTATION— OUTLINING

Instructional Objectives

Students will work collaboratively to:

- Identify the five main points that will be made in a presentation (one per slide).
- Create a new Web-based presentation file for an online working group.
- Invite collaborators to a document.
- Create six slides (one title and five for the main points).
- Create and enter a title for each slide.
- Discuss the possible content for Slides 2 through 6 (e.g., title, text, caption, and image).
- Notify all group members when additional ideas are added to the document.

Time frame: 30–35 minutes

Structure: groups of 3–4 students

IRA/NCTE Standards

Standard 5—Students employ a wide range of strategies as they write and use different writing process elements appropriately to communicate with different audiences for a variety of purposes.

Standard 8—Students use a variety of technological and information resources (e.g., libraries, databases, computer networks, video) to gather and synthesize information and to create and communicate knowledge.

NETS*S Standards

Standard 2. Communication and Collaboration—Students use digital media and environments to communicate and work collaboratively, including at a distance, to support individual learning and contribute to the learning of others.

Standard 3. Research and Information Fluency—Students apply digital tools to gather, evaluate, and use information.

Framework for 21st Century Learning

Communication and Collaboration—Demonstrate ability to work effectively and respectfully with diverse teams.

Use and Manage Information—Manage the flow of information from a wide variety of sources.

Materials/Hardware/Software

- Student Activity Page (one copy per student)

- Brainstorming document from Lesson 17, Planning a Web-Based Presentation—Brainstorming

- One Internet-connected desktop or laptop computer per student

Teacher Preparation

Prior to teaching this lesson, you need to do the following:

1. Add the URL for the Web-based application site to the Student Activity Page before duplicating that page.

2. Add the teacher's user name and user names for the students who worked together in groups to complete Lesson 17, Planning a Web-Based Presentation—Brainstorming, to the Student Activity Page before duplicating that page.

3. Arrange for each student to have access to one Internet-connected desktop or laptop computer for this activity. This may require scheduling lab time or borrowing a laptop cart.

Prerequisite Student Skills

Students need to know how to:

1. Log in to the Web-based application site

2. Create a new presentation file and add slides

3. Add titles to slides

Vocabulary

Web-based presentation tool: Like more traditional presentation tools, these Web-based applications can be used to create, edit, and store presentation slides. Unlike off-line presentation tools, files can be accessed from any Internet-connected computer because they are stored online. In addition, a presentation's creator can share the file with other users, granting viewing or full collaboration rights. Although each Web-based presentation tool will have some unique features, nearly all offer the same basic capabilities for creating and editing slide shows.

Teaching Tips

- This activity is the second of three that demonstrate the power of the collaborative features of Web-based word processing and Web-based presentation tools. You can repeat this series of lessons multiple times using different topics.

- As students review the brainstorming document from Lesson 17, encourage them to think about the best way to organize their ideas to create a five-slide presentation (not including presentation title slide). Remind them that these ideas will lead to the slide titles that will serve as an outline for the presentation.

- Go through this activity yourself before assigning it to students. This will help you anticipate problems that might arise.

Activities/Procedures

1. **Accessing the Web-Based Application Site**—Distribute the Student Activity Page. Ask students to open the Web browser and use the URL written on the activity sheet to navigate to the Web-based application site. (approximately 5 minutes)

2. **Reviewing the Brainstorming Document**—Reunite students who worked together in groups to complete Lesson 17. Direct members of the working groups to review their brainstorming document. Facilitate each group as they identify the points they will cover in their group presentation. (approximately 10 minutes)

3. **Creating the Presentation File**—Make sure each working group chooses one member to set up a presentation file. Remind that person to add group members and you as collaborators. While that person is creating the file, assign remaining group members to discuss titles for Slides 2 through 6. Once the file is created, the typist is to insert the slide titles identified by the group. Slide 1 should include the title of the presentation and the first names of group members. (approximately 10 minutes)

4. **Discussing the Content**—In the remaining time for this activity, ask students to begin discussing the possible content for each slide. Will the slide include a graphic and notes, bulleted items, or other text? Students may take notes in their brainstorming document during this portion of the activity. (up to 10 minutes)

Assessment/Evaluation

- Monitor students while they are working.

- Check each team presentation file for the correct setup (six slides).

- Review the title outlines for each presentation for continuity and content.

Follow-up Activities

- This activity can be repeated whenever students need to outline a presentation.

- The next activity in this sequence leads students through adding images, text, and notes.

Meeting the Needs of Diverse Learners

You might find that students with different abilities will benefit from extra help or extra challenges.

- Except in cases where team dynamics make a change in groupings necessary, keeping the working teams uniform throughout this series of activities will provide support to students who might need extra help.

- Students who would benefit from extra challenges can experiment with features not covered in these activities. For example, they could try rearranging slide order, inserting shapes or drawings, and/or importing slides from an existing PowerPoint file.

Recommended Internet Sites

- Google Docs (http://docs.google.com)

- Zoho (http://zoho.com)

- Presentation Zen blog (http://presentationzen.blogs.com)
  Use this resource yourself to find tips and tricks for creating effective presentations. Share these ideas with students.

Answer Key

Answers will vary depending upon the topic assigned and the main ideas identified. Accept all reasonable responses.

PLANNING A WEB-BASED PRESENTATION— OUTLINING

Objectives

During this activity, you will collaborate with a working group to:

- Review the group's brainstorming document to identify the five main points that will be made in this presentation (one per slide).

- Create a new Web-based presentation file for an online working group.

- Invite collaborators to a document.

- Create six slides (one title and five for the main points).

- Create and enter a title for each slide.

- Discuss possible content for Slides 2 through 6. For example, will a slide include an image, bullet points, and/or notes?

- Notify all group members when additional ideas are added to the document.

Before You Begin

When planning a presentation, brainstormed ideas have to be organized into topics, subtopics, and details. Identifying the main ideas you want to cover and deciding their order is an important part of creating a slide show. When your presentation is viewed by an audience, the slide sequence should move logically from one point to the next.

Slide titles can be used as a kind of outline to organize thoughts in a way that makes sense. That allows viewers to follow along easily. Pre-planning also helps determine what content needs to be included on each slide and the most effective format to use. For example, can an image get a point across? Is additional text needed on the slide (besides the title)? What narration needs to be added to each slide's notes area?

Complete this activity with your working team. You may use this activity to create a presentation in a working group on another day.

Materials

- Student Activity Page (one copy per student)

- Web-based application URL: _____

- Teacher's user name: _____

- User names for classmate collaborators: _____

  _____

- Brainstorming document created in Lesson 17, Planning a Web-Based Presentation—Brainstorming

Directions

Accessing the Web-Based Application Site

Use the URL written on this activity sheet to navigate to the Web-based application site and log in.

Reviewing the Brainstorming Document

1. Open the brainstorming document your group created in Lesson 17, Planning a Web-Based Presentation—Brainstorming.

2. Review and refine ideas.

3. Work with your group to identify the points you want to cover in your presentation.

Creating the Presentation File

1. Choose one member of your group to set up a presentation file and add collaborators.

2. While your group typist is creating the file, discuss titles for Slides 2 through 6 with your group members.

3. Once the file is created, have the group typist add the titles identified by the group. Include on Slide 1 the title of the presentation and the first names of group members.

Discussing the Content

1. As a group, discuss what content will be included on Slides 2 through 6. Will there be a graphic and notes, bulleted items, or other text?

2. As you plan, make notes in your group's brainstorming document.

3. If you add additional notes or ideas to your group documents later, notify the collaborators.

19 PLANNING A WEB-BASED PRESENTATION— IMAGES AND TEXT

Instructional Objectives

Students will work collaboratively to:

- Write a short script (two to three sentences) for each slide to add to the slides' Notes areas.

- Decide on the formats for Slides 2 through 6 (e.g., title and text, caption and image).

- Determine who will be responsible for completing Slides 2 through 6 and adding the script.

- Complete Slides 2 through 6.

- Notify all group members when individual work is done.

Time frame: one class period

Structure: groups of 3–4 students

IRA/NCTE Standards

Standard 5—Students employ a wide range of strategies as they write and use different writing process elements appropriately to communicate with different audiences for a variety of purposes.

Standard 8—Students use a variety of technological and information resources (e.g., libraries, databases, computer networks, video) to gather and synthesize information and to create and communicate knowledge.

NETS*S Standards

Standard 2. Communication and Collaboration—Students use digital media and environments to communicate and work collaboratively, including at a distance, to support individual learning and contribute to the learning of others.

Standard 3. Research and Information Fluency—Students apply digital tools to gather, evaluate, and use information.

Framework for 21st Century Learning

Communication and Collaboration—Demonstrate ability to work effectively and respectfully with diverse teams.

Use and Manage Information—Manage the flow of information from a wide variety of sources.

Materials/Hardware/Software

- Student Activity Page (one copy per student)

- Student outlines from Lesson 18, Planning a Web-Based Presentation—Outlining

- Collection of digital images (provided by teacher)

- One Internet-connected desktop or laptop computer per student

Teacher Preparation

Prior to teaching this lesson, you need to do the following:

1. Add the URL for the Web-based application site to the Student Activity Page before duplicating that page.

2. Gather and provide a collection of digital images related to the assigned topic for students to choose from to insert on slides as needed. These photos may be posted online or stored on each student's desktop or laptop computer hard drive. Add the collection's URL or access directions to the Student Activity Page before duplicating that page.

3. Decide if you want groups to publish their final presentations. This allows groups to view one another's files without being able to edit them. If files are published, students need to provide the URL to you.

4. Arrange for each student to have access to one Internet-connected desktop or laptop computer for this activity. This may require scheduling lab time or borrowing a laptop cart.

Prerequisite Student Skills

Students need to know how to:

1. Log in to the Web-based application site

2. Access an existing presentation file

3. Insert images on a slide

4. Add notes to a slide

Vocabulary

Web-based presentation tool: Like more traditional presentation tools, these Web-based applications can be used to create, edit, and store presentation slides. Unlike off-line presentation tools, files can be accessed from any Internet-connected computer because they are stored online. In addition, a presentation's creator can share the file with other users, granting viewing or full collaboration rights. Although each Web-based presentation tool will have some unique features, nearly all offer the same basic capabilities for creating and editing slide shows.

Teaching Tips

- This activity is the last in a series of three that demonstrates the power of the collaborative features of Web-based word processing and Web-based presentation tools. Work that is not completed in class may be assigned as homework.

- Once students are familiar with this process, they can complete most or all future assignments of this type of work as homework, as long as they have access to Internet-connected computers outside of school.

- Go through this activity yourself before assigning it to students. This will help you anticipate problems that might arise.

Activities/Procedures

1. **Accessing the Web-Based Application Site**—Distribute the Student Activity Page. Ask students to open the Web browser and use the URL written on the activity sheet to navigate to the Web-based application site. (approximately 5 minutes)

2. **Writing a Short Script**—Ask groups to review the titles added to each slide created in Lesson 18, Planning a Web-Based Presentation—Outlining, then work together to develop a short script for the presentation. Students will add this script to the Notes area of each slide. Students should only write two to three sentences per slide to provide the narrative for the presenter(s) when the slide show is shared with a group. As the group members write the script, they determine the visual and text content for each slide (e.g., image and title, bulleted text items). (approximately 25 minutes)

3. **Working on the Presentation**—Remind students that every group member must be responsible for some aspect of the work. Ask each working group to determine how they will complete Slides 2 through 6, then do the necessary work (slide content and adding relevant script sentences to the Notes area for each slide). Show students how to access the digital image collection. When they have finished, individual students are to send notifications to the other members of the working group. If appropriate, the group may publish its presentation file when completed and give you the URL. (approximately 30 minutes)

Assessment/Evaluation

- Monitor students while they are working.

- Check the slide content for each presentation file for accuracy and clarity.

- Check the Notes area for each slide to read the script.

Follow-up Activities

This activity can be repeated along with the previous two activities whenever students need to work collaboratively on a presentation.

Meeting the Needs of Diverse Learners

You might find that students with different abilities will benefit from extra help or extra challenges.

- Except in cases where team dynamics make a change in groupings necessary, keeping the working teams uniform throughout this series of activities will provide support to students who might need extra help. Some students may prefer to dictate the script to a classmate who will write down the sentences. Other students may prefer to work on paper and then enter their notes.

- Students who would benefit from extra challenges can experiment with features not covered in these activities. For example, they could try changing slide backgrounds, using slide templates, or using other methods for viewing completed presentations.

Recommended Internet Sites

- Google Docs (http://docs.google.com)
- Zoho (http://zoho.com)

Answer Key

Answers will vary. Accept all reasonable responses.

19 PLANNING A WEB-BASED PRESENTATION— IMAGES AND TEXT

Objective

During this activity, you will collaborate with your working group to write a short script for the group presentation you created in Lesson 18, Planning a Web-Based Presentation— Outlining. You will also add images and text to complete Slides 2 through 6.

Before You Begin

To keep slide shows interesting, presenters think very carefully about what they want to say and how they want to say it. Slide shows should use as little text on each slide as possible. Images help get points across at a glance. One good strategy is to write a script. This helps presenters to explain fully ideas that they briefly state on each slide.

In short presentations, the script often consists of just a few sentences for each slide. The appropriate sentences are added to each slide's Notes area.

Complete this activity with your working team. Use the brainstorming and outlining work you have done in prior activities to help you.

Materials

- Student Activity Page (one copy per student)

- Outline from Lesson 18, Planning a Web-Based Presentation—Outlining

- Web-based application URL: _____

- URL for digital image collection (provided by your teacher) or directions for how to access these files: _____

Directions

Accessing the Web-Based Application Site

Use the URL written on this activity sheet to navigate to the Web-based application site and log in.

Writing a Short Script

1. Review the titles your group added to each slide during the previous activity. Use these titles as an outline.

2. Work with your group to develop a short script for the presentation. This script should include two to three sentences for each slide.

3. As you write the script, decide what each slide will look like. For example, will the slide have an image and title? Or, will it have text items (no more than three bullets)?

Working on the Presentation

1. As a team, decide what each member will do to complete the presentation, and then do the work.

2. Add content to each slide and type the script sentences for individual slides into the Notes area.

3. Remember to use the digital image collection provided by your teacher for those slides where you want to insert images.

4. When you are finished with your part of the work, send notifications to the other members of your group.

5. If your teacher asks your group to publish its presentation file, give the URL to your teacher.

20 SIX-WORD STORIES

Instructional Objectives

Students will work collaboratively to:

- Create a presentation file that includes 1 six-word story per group member.

- Notify all group members when individual work is done.

Time frame: approximately 45 minutes

Structure: groups of 3–4 students

IRA/NCTE Standards

Standard 4—Students adjust their use of spoken, written, and visual language (e.g., conventions, style, vocabulary) to communicate effectively with a variety of audiences and for different purposes.

Standard 8—Students use a variety of technological and information resources (e.g., libraries, databases, computer networks, video) to gather and synthesize information and to create and communicate knowledge.

NETS*S Standards

Standard 1. Creativity and Innovation —Students demonstrate creative thinking, construct knowledge, and develop innovative products and processes using technology.

Standard 2. Communication and Collaboration—Students use digital media and environments to communicate and work collaboratively, including at a distance, to support individual learning and contribute to the learning of others.

Framework for 21st Century Learning

Communication and Collaboration—Demonstrate ability to work effectively and respectfully with diverse teams.

Materials/Hardware/Software

- Student Activity Page (one copy per student)

- Collection of digital images (provided by teacher)

- One Internet-connected desktop or laptop computer per student

Teacher Preparation

Prior to teaching this lesson, you need to do the following:

1. Choose a broad topic for six-word stories. This might be related to assigned reading or to a current event.

2. Create working groups of 3–4 students and provide the students' working group assignments prior to beginning the activity.

3. Add the URL for the Web-based application site, the teacher's user name, and user names for classmate collaborators to the Student Activity Page before duplicating that page.

4. Provide a collection of digital images related to the assigned topic that students may use to illustrate their story. You may post these photos online or store them on each student's desktop or laptop hard drive. Add the collection's URL or access directions to the Student Activity Page.

5. Arrange for each student to have access to one Internet-connected desktop or laptop computer for this activity. This may require scheduling lab time or borrowing a laptop cart.

Prerequisite Student Skills

Students need to know how to:

1. Log in to the Web-based application site

2. Create a new presentation file

3. Insert images on a slide

4. Add text to a slide

Vocabulary

Web-based presentation tool: Like more traditional presentation tools, these Web-based applications can be used to create, edit, and store presentation slides. Unlike off-line presentation tools, files can be accessed from any Internet-connected computer because they are stored online. In addition, a presentation's creator can share the file with other users, granting viewing or full collaboration rights. Although each Web-based presentation tool will have some unique features, nearly all offer the same basic capabilities for creating and editing slide shows.

Teaching Tips

- This activity encourages students to think creatively about how they will tell a story and work with others to create a presentation file that includes three or four stories.

- Work that is not completed in class may be assigned as homework.

- Go through this activity yourself before assigning it to students. This will help you anticipate problems that might arise.

Activities/Procedures

1. **Introducing the Six-Word Story**—Distribute the Student Activity Page. Tell students that author Ernest Hemingway once wrote a story that consisted of just six words: "For sale: baby shoes, never worn." Explain that students will each write a six-word story about a topic you assign and add the story to a Web-based presentation file created for this purpose. They will share the file with two or three other students. Ask students to open the Web browser and use the URL written on the activity sheet to navigate to the Web-based application site. (approximately 5 minutes)

2. **Creating the Presentation File**—Each working group chooses one member to set up a presentation file and add collaborators (working group members and teacher). This student also adds the title for this presentation, "Six-Word Stories," to the first slide along with the first names of group members. While the typist creates the file, remaining group members discuss ideas for six-word stories on the assigned topic. (approximately 10 minutes)

3. **Writing the Stories**—Once the file is created, each student inserts a slide for his or her story. After adding the text for the story, students may review the image collection you have provided to illustrate their story. When they have finished, individual students send you a notification. If appropriate, the group may publish its presentation file when completed and give you the URL. (approximately 30 minutes)

Assessment/Evaluation

- Monitor students while they are working.

- Check each student's slide to ensure that the story meets the assignment criteria, including that the story is about the assigned topic and consists of just six words.

Follow-up Activities

- This activity can be repeated using different topics.

- Students can create longer stories using more slides.

117

Meeting the Needs of Diverse Learners

You might find that students with different abilities will benefit from extra help or extra challenges.

- Students who need extra help will benefit from working through this activity on paper before working online. Also, because the document is online, these students can continue to practice these skills anywhere they have access to the Internet.

- Students who would benefit from extra challenges can experiment with simulating text animations by using two to three slides to tell their stories.

Recommended Internet Sites

- Google Docs (http://docs.google.com)
- Zoho (http://zoho.com)

Answer Key

Answers will vary. Accept all reasonable responses.

20 SIX-WORD STORIES

Objective

During this activity, you will collaborate with your working group to create a presentation file that includes one six-word story per group member. Individuals will notify all group members when their work is done.

Before You Begin

Author Ernest Hemingway once wrote a six-word story: "For sale: baby shoes, never worn."

In this activity, you will write a six-word story about a topic assigned by your teacher and add the story to a group Web-based presentation file.

Complete this activity with your assigned working team.

Materials

- Student Activity Page (one copy per student)

- Web-based application URL: _____

- Teacher's user name: _____

- User names for group members: _____

- URL for digital image collection (provided by your teacher) or directions for how to access these files: _____

_____

Directions

Creating the Presentation File

1. Open the Web browser. Use the URL written on this activity sheet to navigate to the Web-based application site. Log in.

2. Choose one member of your group to set up a presentation file and add collaborators (your working group members and your teacher).

3. The typist also adds the title for this presentation, "Six-Word Stories," to the first slide, along with the first names of group members.

4. While the typist is creating the file, remaining group members discuss ideas for six-word stories on the assigned topic.

Writing the Stories

1. Insert a slide for your story in the group's presentation file.

2. Add the text for your story.

3. Review the image collection provided by your teacher. Choose an image to illustrate your story and insert it on your slide.

4. When you finish, send a notification to your teacher.

5. If your teacher asks your group to publish its presentation file, give the URL to your teacher.

APPENDIX

Lesson 1: Working in a Wiki

Create a class wiki. Use the Front Page to establish the purpose of the wiki and to set up Sidebar links to pages you create for each activity.

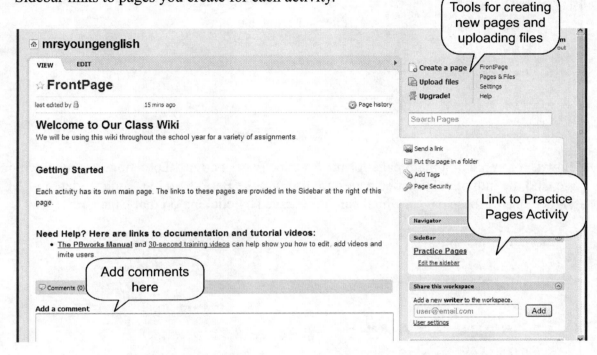

Every wiki allows users to upload different types of files. In this lesson, you need to upload a digital image that students will insert on their practice pages.

This screen shot shows the list of files that have been uploaded to this sample wiki.

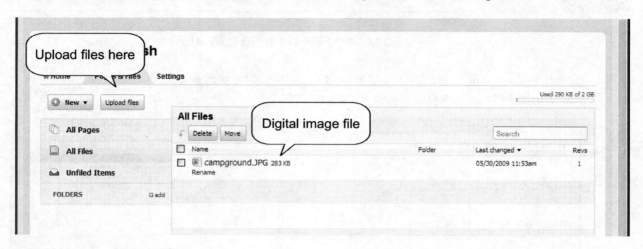

Below is a sample of a main page for the Practice Pages activity. Directions are included on this page, and the individual practice pages are listed in the Period 1 table. Each student in Period 1 is assigned one of these pages, which can be accessed by clicking on that page name.

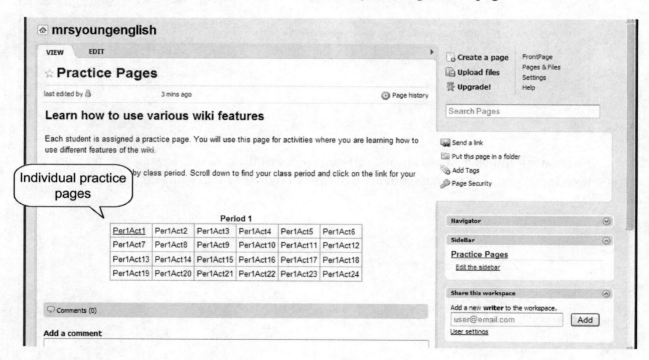

This is a sample of an individual practice page. This is where students will add text and insert a digital image.

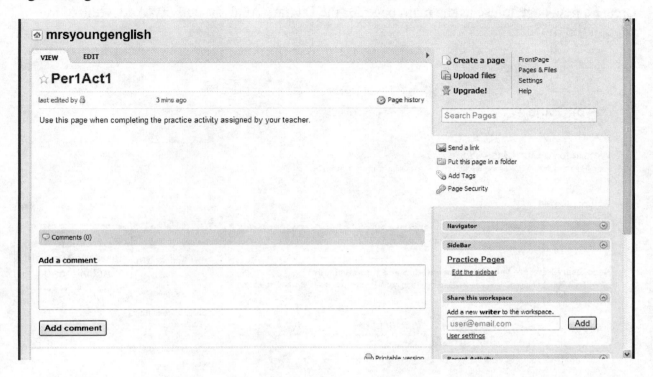

Lesson 2: Literary Analysis—21st Century Style

Create a new page to use as the main page for the Literary Analysis activity. Add a link to this page in the Sidebar.

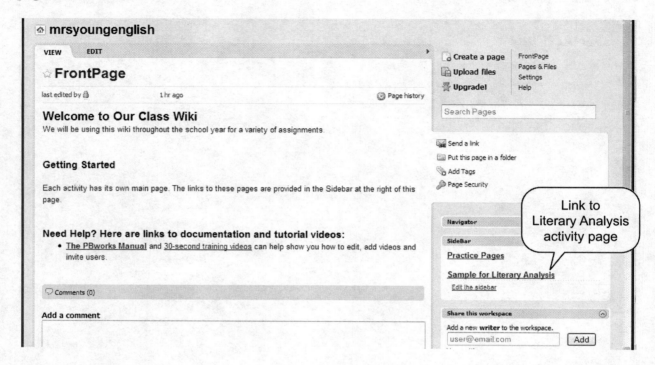

This is a sample of a main page for the Literary Analysis activity. Directions are included on this page, and the individual practice pages are listed in the Period 1 table. Each team in Period 1 is assigned one of these pages, which can be accessed by clicking on that page name.

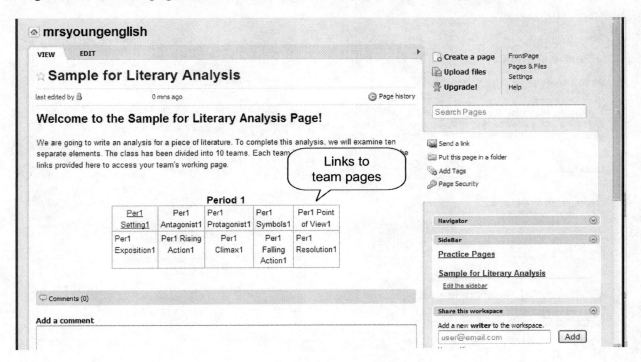

This is a sample of a team work page. This is where teams will add their definitions, descriptions, and explanations.

Lesson 3: Build Your Own Reference Library—Glossary of Terms

Create a new page to use as the main page for the Glossary of Terms activity. Add a link to this page in the Sidebar.

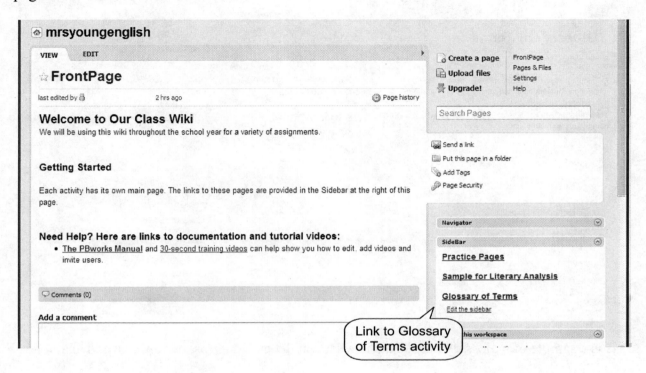

Link to Glossary of Terms activity

This is a sample of a main page for the Glossary of Terms activity. The purpose of this section of the wiki is provided here, along with links to individual glossary pages.

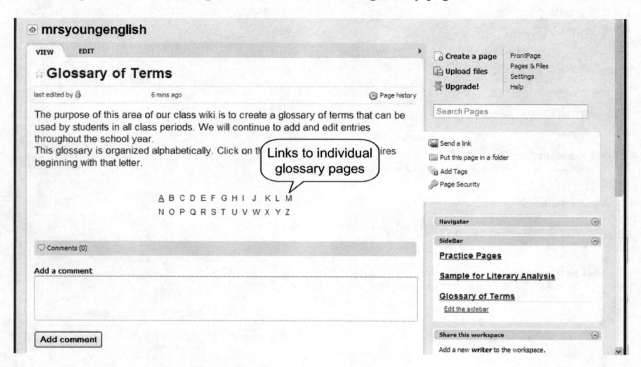

This is a sample of a glossary page. This is where students add terms, definitions, and examples.

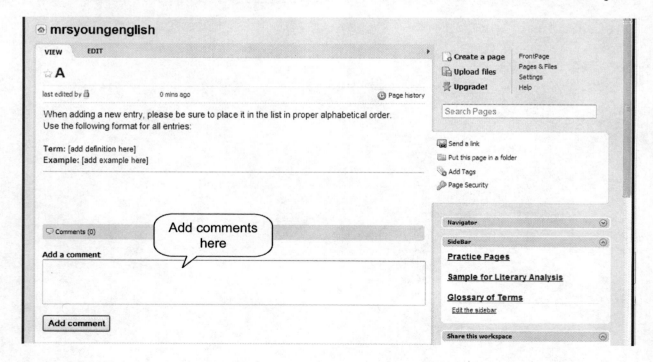

Lesson 4: Build Your Own Reference Library—Formatting and Style Guide

Create a new page to use as the main page for the Formatting and Style Guide activity. Add a link to this page in the Sidebar.

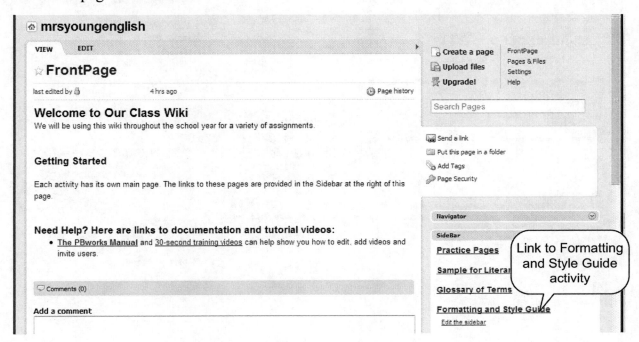

This is a sample of a main page for the Formatting and Style Guide activity. The purpose of this section of the wiki is provided here, along with links to individual guide pages.

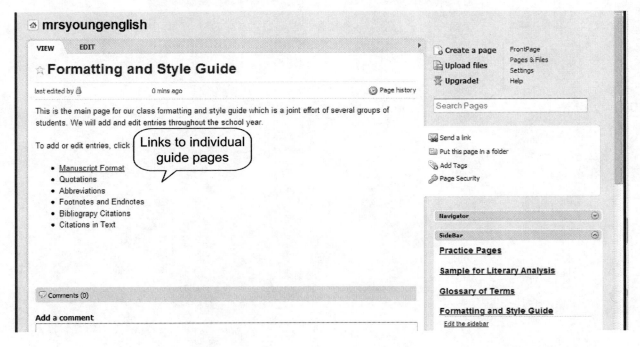

This is a sample of a formatting and style guide page. This is where students add entries and examples.

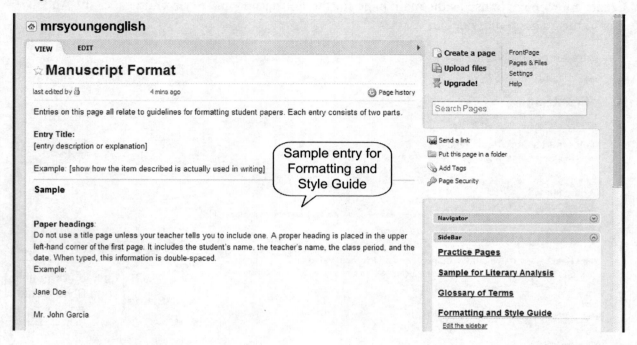

Lesson 5: Read All About It

Create a new page to use as the main page for the Book Review activity. Add a link to this page in the Sidebar.

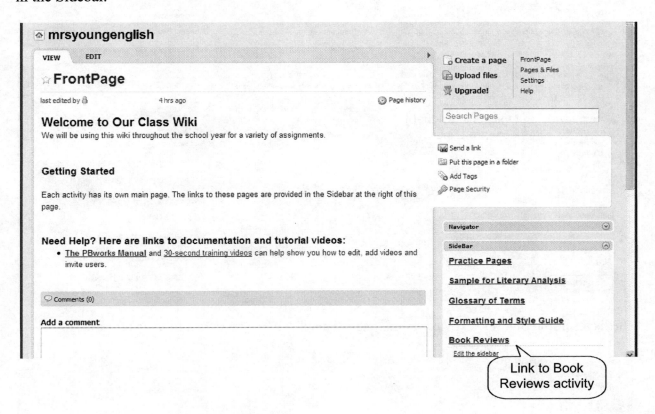

Link to Book Reviews activity

This is a sample of a main page for the Book Review activity. The purpose of this section of the wiki is provided here along with links to individual genre pages.

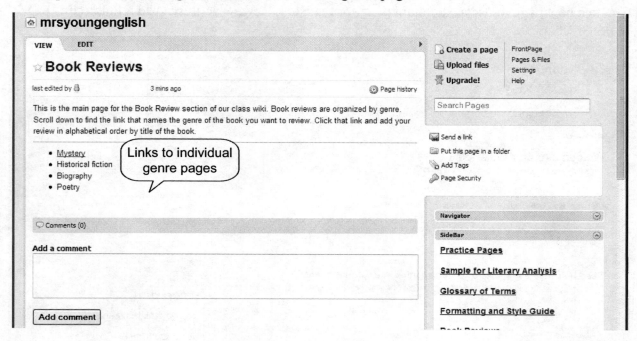

This is a sample of a book review genre page. This is where students add their reviews.

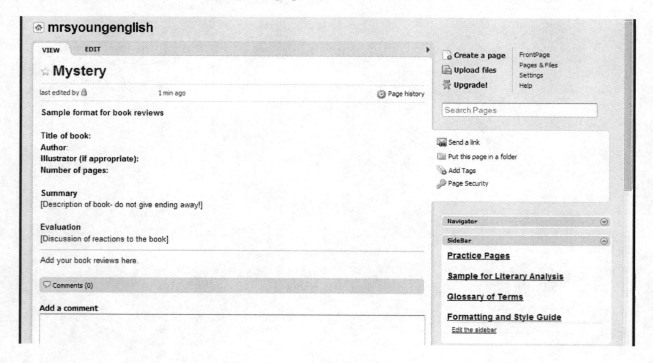

Lesson 6: Working in a Blog

Create a class blog. Use the About area to establish the purpose of the blog.

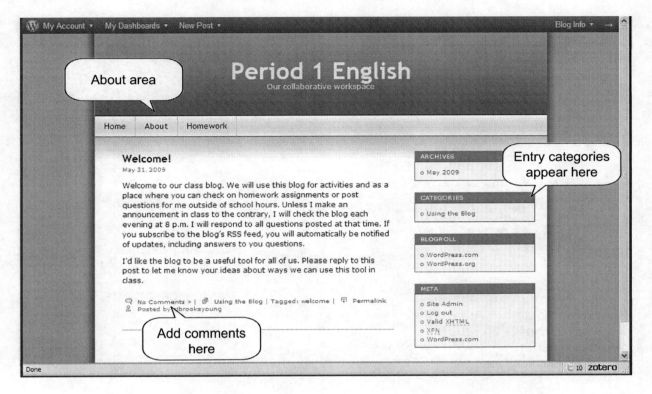

Lesson 7: Poetry Anthology

Sample entry for Poetry Anthology lesson:

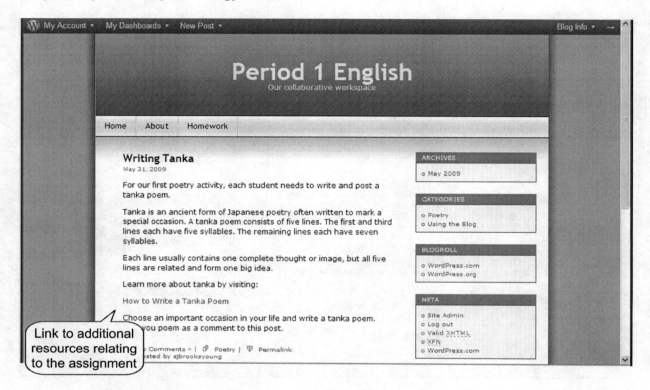

Lesson 8: What a Character!

Sample entry for What a Character! lesson:

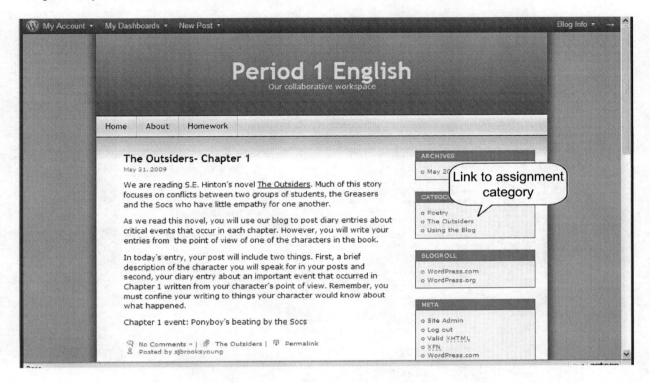

Lesson 9: Book Study

Sample entry for Book Study lesson:

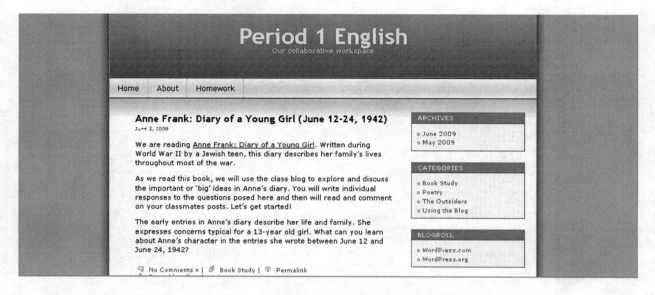

Lesson 10: Interactive News

Sample entry for Interactive News lesson:

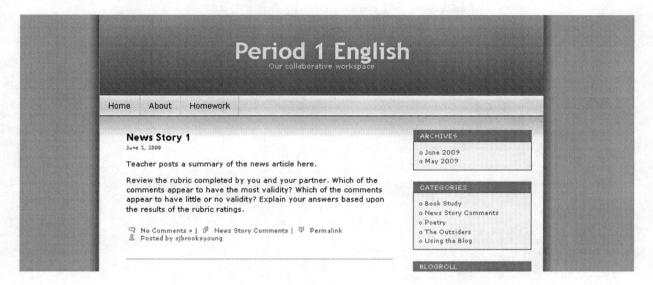

Lesson 11: Using a Web-Based Word Processor
Lesson 12: Collaborative Notes
Lesson 13: Writing a Mini-Essay
Lesson 14: Peer Editing a Mini-Essay
Lesson 15: Revising a Mini-Essay

Sample document for Lessons 11 through 15:

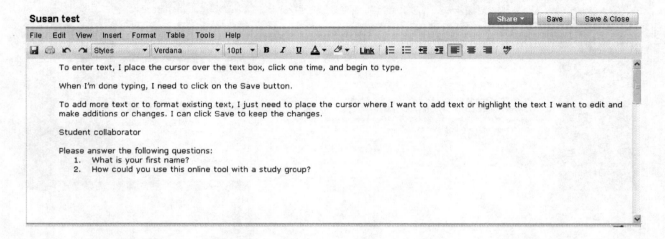

Lesson 16: Using a Web-Based Presentation Tool
Lesson 17: Planning a Web-Based Presentation—Brainstorming
Lesson 18: Planning a Web-Based Presentation—Outlining
Lesson 19: Planning a Web-Based Presentation—Images and Text
Lesson 20: Six-Word Stories

Sample presentation for Lessons 16 through 20. Students will add slides, images, and notes as appropriate.

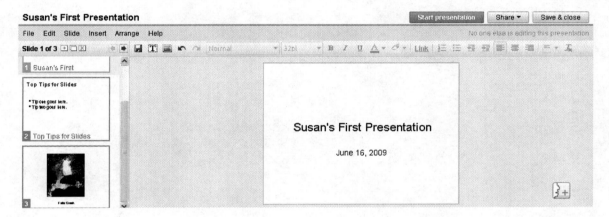